The Forgotten Room

The Forgotten Room

Inside a Public Alternative School for At-Risk Youth

Mary Hollowell

LEXINGTON BOOKS

A division of

ROWMAN & LITTLEFIELD PUBLISHERS, INC.
Lanham • Boulder • New York • Toronto • Plymouth, UK

KH

Published by Lexington Books
A division of Rowman & Littlefield Publishers, Inc.
A wholly owned subsidary of The Rowman & Littlefield Publishing Group, Inc.
4501 Forbes Boulevard, Suite 200, Lanham, Maryland 20706
http://www.lexingtonbooks.com

Estover Road,
Plymouth PL6 7PY
United Kingdom

British Library Cataloguing in Publication Information Available

Library of Congress Cataloging-in-Publication Data

Hollowell, Mary, 1964–
  The forgotten room : inside a public alternative school for at-risk youth / Mary
Hollowell.
     p. cm.
  Includes bibliographical references and index.
  ISBN 978-0-7391-3495-5 (cloth : alk. paper) — ISBN 978-0-7391-3497-9 (electronic)
  1. Children with social disabilities—Education (Middle school)—Georgia—Case
studies. 2. Alternative schools—Georgia—Case studies. 3. Middle schools—Georgia—
Case studies. I. Title.
  LC4092.G4H65 2010
  371.9'0473—dc22   2009027472

Printed in the United States of America

∞™ The paper used in this publication meets the minimum requirements of American
National Standard for Information Sciences—Permanence of Paper for Printed Library
Materials, ANSI/NISO Z39.48-1992.

10/4/11

Contents

Foreword by Ashley Bryan   vii

Chapter One   August   1

Chapter Two   September   9

Chapter Three   October   31

Chapter Four   November   53

Chapter Five   December   79

Chapter Six   January   97

Chapter Seven   February   109

Chapter Eight   March   123

Chapter Nine   April   141

Chapter Ten   May   153

Epilogue   163

Author's Note: Reflections on Alternative Schooling   167

Bibliography   175

Index   177

About the Author   181

Foreword

Ashley Bryan

Professor Mary Evelyn Hollowell has had an extensive career in education. She brings her experience to bear in this journal, a documentation of her year in a rural alternative school in Georgia. It is a gripping account. One is moved by the courage with which Professor Hollowell faced the daily challenges that are described in this journal.

Wherever Prof. Hollowell has taught, she has invited me to share my work with her students. She arranged my visit to this school. I came prepared, as always, to reach the audience through my program of Black American poets, Black American spirituals, and African tales. I engaged the students in an active participation by leading them in chanting lines of poems after me. This opened the students to the vocal play evoked by the printed words of the poem. This led to my retelling of African tales in which I use the devices of poetry. The students helped with the story by call and response interaction. I closed with the music of Black American spirituals.

The program was warmly received. I felt I had elicited as helpful and warm a response from the students as I had from any other audience. I was not aware of the possibility of disruption, as described as an on-going challenge to the teachers of this school. Prof. Hollowell describes the teachers' handling of difficult situations as they arose. She recognized the caring approach of the teachers. She observed them in class and noted their strategies for moving forward with the required subject matter. On occasions when she substituted, she followed the example of the best of the sessions she had observed or in which she had taken part. She held steadily to her belief that the nonconfrontational approach would lead to positive changes in the students' growth.

In the midfifties, I taught in an alternative school. The Wiltwyck School for Boys, 9-13 years old, was in upstate Esopus, New York. These students had been in trouble that had brought them into court. The judge then assigned them to this school setting for rehabilitation. The midfifties posed less of a problem to a teacher in an alternative school than what a teacher faces today. There was not the same concern of guns, knives, security checks, or the level of violence that is common in our society today.

I worked in the art studio, directed by the art therapist, Edith Kramer. Her book *Art Therapy in a Children's Community* has become a basic book for educators and art teachers. In conference with the staff, Ms. Kramer would contribute insights into possible forthcoming changes in the student that she noted the art predicted. When Ms. Kramer saw how well I worked with the students, she left me in midyear to devote her time to completing her book. I had no training in interpreting students' art work. I worked only to open the esthetic challenge of whatever the student was painting. Problems were minor, although I had been advised that I would have help in removing a disruptive student from the setting, if necessary. I was able to follow Ms. Kramer's lead and get fine artwork from the students.

Like the Wiltwyck staff, Professor Hollowell believes in the constructive outreach to all students. She was completely unprepared for the shock of discovering that there was a solitary confinement cell located in the rural alternative school she was documenting. It was hard for her to grasp that the teachers whose compassion and restraint she had noted in their dealing with the students would allow for such a practice.

Since then, Professor Hollowell has become active with other educators and parents in condemning these solitary confinement cells. They have joined together in working toward the elimination of these confinement cells in public schools, wherever they exist in states across the country.

Clearly, Prof. Hollowell believes in educational reform and the ongoing efforts to reach students with problems. It is her hope that these students will also become contributors to our society.

Chapter 1

AUGUST

AUGUST 5

"These are tough kids," the principal told me three times on the phone and, again, during my job interview. Students were sent to Peachtree Alternative School for assaulting teachers, sexually harassing peers, bringing weapons to school, and making terroristic threats. They had also dealt drugs, committed burglary and vandalism, and were chronically disruptive. Most of the students were boys, and most were on parole. Half were black, and half were white.

I was interviewing for the middle school science teacher position. I had just moved to Georgia and was anxious for a job. Midsummer was a bad time to begin looking for a teaching spot since most new teachers had already been hired. Peachtree Alternative was the only school left that had an opening in my field.

One of my friends taught at an alternative school in Milwaukee, and I had visited her classes. Her alternative school was unusual in that it had a relaxed atmosphere and a lot of student input into the curriculum. Students chose their own books and projects. They even graded their teacher's performance.

My friend's school was hardly a boot camp. Teachers, there, viewed themselves more as therapists than jailers. They wore blue jeans, and students called them by their first names. Teachers barely even raised their voices. The Milwaukee students, some of the toughest kids in the city, did community service, participated in school governance, and received academic credit for work-study opportunities. Many of them graduated.

I wondered if this nonpunitive philosophy of alternative schooling would extend to a rural community in the Deep South.

Mary Henderson, the principal of Peachtree Alternative, peered at me over the top of her bifocals, which were secured by a chain around her neck. She wore a tee

1

Figure 1.   The Front Entrance to the School.

shirt that said "Grandma" beneath a blue-jean jumper that, as experienced teachers know, is a practical school uniform. Jumpers let you to bend and stretch without exposing skin, and they provide good ventilation on hot summer afternoons.

My other interviewer was Louise Bates, the high school English teacher. She was an attractive woman with a big smile and snow white hair. The two women looked at me expectantly. "What do you think of the building?" Ms. Henderson asked.

"Well," I stammered, getting ready to confess that I thought it was pretty grim. The two women started laughing. Ms. Henderson, herself, had indicated during our phone conversation that the building was a dump.

It was a decrepit structure from the 1950s that had been abandoned for a while, before it was reopened in the late nineties as an alternative school. The paint was peeling, the walls were crumbling, and floor tiles were missing. Broken windows were either boarded up or the cracks were patched with duct tape. A blue dumpster beside the front door welcomed visitors. The gutters were rusted and collapsing, and rust streaked the sides of the building. Weeds grew along the base of the building, and the parking lot had huge potholes.

Across the street, a graffiti-covered gymnasium had a front lawn strewn with bits of paper, broken glass, and crushed beer cans. A few chickens pecked around in the red dirt.

I had visited dilapidated schools in American inner cities and schools in rural Kenya with no electricity or running water. Even by those standards,

Peachtree Alternative School was shoddy. Apparently, Ms. Henderson and Ms. Bates agreed. The principal told me about her struggle to maintain the building. "This old building is expensive," she said. "The roof leaks, and we've probably had to repair the air conditioner about fifty times. I do have a fully staffed cafeteria."

The interview began in earnest. "We have kids who'll spit at you, swear at you, knock you down," said Ms. Bates. "How would you handle these students?"

I was shocked. "Do they really spit at you?" I asked. Spitting was an ultimate form of disrespect.

"Well, not that much," Ms. Bates conceded.

I answered the question by babbling about the importance of being over-prepared. "Always have a backup plan," I said. "Use a variety of methods to teach a diversity of learners."

I remembered the advice that Martin Haberman gave in his 1995 book *Star Teachers of Children in Poverty*. Haberman was one of my heroes. I'd read all of his books and heard him speak on several occasions. I knew that Peachtree Alternative students, in that rural community, were likely to be poor. I echoed Haberman, saying that being flexible, admitting my own mistakes, and having respect for parents were other means of handling students.

"What would you do," asked Ms. Henderson, "on day one when you were faced with fifteen hyperactive children? What would your classroom management strategy be?"

The term "classroom management" threw me for a loop for a few seconds. I knew that many alternative students had lives so punishing, so filled with poverty, crime, abuse, and addiction, that they were almost immune to punishment. Few punishments that teachers gave would make a difference. A system of rewards would be more useful, as would role modeling good behavior, circulating around the room, and ignoring minor misbehaviors until they extinguished themselves.

"It's important to know students' names, right away," I told the women. "Get to know as much about their lives as you can. The more you know about them, the better your discipline will be. It'd be ideal if we could visit every student at home, get to know parents, although I know that's not possible."

I paused to catch my breath. "Incorporate your own interests into teaching," I added. "Let them see you outside the classroom, in different contexts."

I told the women that I had a lot of practical experience in science, ranging from working in a museum to a zoo to a marine biology lab. "I have a lot of stories that enliven my teaching," I told them. I also felt compelled to explain why I'd had so many different jobs over the years, "My husband was in television news, so we moved around a lot. Now, we're more settled."

After hearing about my previous employers, Ms. Henderson asked, "Why would someone like you, with your museum background, be interested in this job?"

I'd anticipated the question. According to my guru, Haberman, saying that I liked children wouldn't be good enough, so I told them, "I love science, and I like challenges." It was true. I *did* love science, and I *did* want to see if I could hack it teaching alternative students, like my friend in Milwaukee. Plus, I'd already checked the pay scale, and I could earn more teaching in a public school than I had at any of my "fun jobs" that paid a pittance.

To demonstrate my love of teaching, I told them about some museum science courses I had taught in Cincinnati. One course, inside a natural history museum, was called The Geological Wonders of Africa, and we handled fluorescent rocks. "I have good ideas leftover from teaching in museums," I said, hoping to entice the women.

Ms. Bates tried to entice me right back. "Ms. Henderson lets us do creative things," she said, which was good news to hear about a principal.

Ms. Henderson told me some about her own background. She was an English teacher, then a counselor, then an administrator at an alternative school in Ohio. "That school was nothing like this one. We had vocational education there," she said, clearly missing her old school. "We can't save every child, but we can save some of them, and we can save some of them through vocational education. Not everyone's meant to go to college."

She had moved to the South, after a divorce, to be closer to her daughter and grandson. Ms. Henderson had been a substitute administrator for a while, then an assistant principal at Peachtree Alternative School for a year before becoming principal. This was her second year as principal. She thought that Ohio public schools were light years ahead of Georgia's in terms of school resources.

Ms. Bates had been in journalism for almost twenty years before becoming an English teacher. She had worked at a newspaper in Arkansas. Her own daughter had been an alternative school student. That was part of her reason for teaching at Peachtree Alternative, and she loved it. "I wouldn't teach anywhere else," she said.

In fact, most of the twelve teachers at Peachtree Alternative were mid-career teachers who had come to alternative schooling from other fields. The wealth of older, veteran teachers was rare. Most alternative schools had young inexperienced teachers and high teacher turnover. Some Peachtree Alternative teachers had been in the military, and others had been in counseling. One teacher had been in gifted education and wanted to apply the same high standards to at-risk youth. Teachers at Peachtree Alternative School were also unusual in that many had taught at the school for three or more years. Some had been teaching there as many as seven, eight, or nine years.

The actual curriculum at Peachtree Alternative School sounded daunting. "These kids need life skills," Ms. Bates told me. "Some of them don't even know how to look you in the eye when they're speaking." I tried to imagine practicing greetings with students.

"Especially those middle schoolers," Ms. Henderson added. "They *really* don't know how to act in the classroom. They're so jumpy. It takes them until October to settle down."

"Your other classes would be earth science for sixth graders, life science for seventh, and physics for eighth," said Ms. Bates. The three different science courses would take a lot of planning, and I wondered if I could get away with varying each class only slightly.

"What's the class size?" I asked.

"The cap is fifteen," said Ms. Henderson. That was larger than the six to eight students per class she had quoted on the phone.

I shook hands with the women and headed out the door. It was the middle of summer, and there were only a few cars in the parking lot. Georgia red clay was everywhere, in large bare patches on the ground and in streaks on the asphalt. It even hung in the air in a reddish haze.

Peachtree Alternative was surrounded by low-rise housing projects and a handful of homes. Some of the homes were made of unpainted concrete. They had boarded-up windows but were still occupied. Other homes were wooden. They had broken steps, sagging front porches, and torn screens. Side lots contained old furniture, rusted appliances, and abandoned cars resting on concrete blocks.

The main road, a block away from the school, had a filling station across from a fried chicken franchise. Beside the filling station was an abandoned restaurant, and beside the fried chicken franchise was a boarded-up building with the words "no loitering" spray painted in big red letters.

As I headed down Rural Route 14, the homes became statelier. Franklin had a town square with a historic brick courthouse, constructed in 1845. Farther down the road was a quaint town called Great Oaks. Its homes had the distinct feel of the Old South with long porches, tall white columns, and yards filled with towering oak trees. I treated myself to lunch at the famed Black Stallion Inn in Great Oaks. As I rocked on the wide front porch and waited for a table, a girl in a hoop skirt and wide-brimmed hat served me lemonade. My lunch was fried chicken, collard greens, and black-eyed peas, but I passed on the pecan pie dessert.

AUGUST 26

I didn't hear about the job until weeks later when I called the school. Ms. Henderson told me that she'd planned to hire me, but the position had been canceled, at the last minute. She apologized profusely. "I'm sorry I didn't call," she said. "We've just been so busy."

The county school budget had been slashed by 3.5 million dollars, and the first thing to go was salaries. Peachtree Alternative School lost five staff members over the summer. The assistant principal, secretary, librarian, full-time nurse, and in-school suspension officer all lost their jobs. It also lost its high school art and physical education programs.

Ms. Henderson said that she almost cried when she heard about the job cuts. "I told the teachers I have left, 'Now, don't be too good or they'll think we don't need any more people.'"

She urged me to be a regular substitute teacher at the school. "I can't get substitutes to come to this school," she said. "They won't set foot in the door, and some of them only have GEDs."

"It's stressful, here," she said, "but I have to laugh or else I'd go crazy. There's a lot of humor around here."

"We're more expensive than other schools," Ms. Henderson said. "We spend twice as much per pupil, and we're only allowed 120 students. We're supposed to have a low student-to-teacher ratio, but this year, our classes are going to be about fifteen to eighteen students. We'll have chronic discipline problems and no room for disaffected youth."

I knew that "disaffected" was a term for quieter students who were more lonely and withdrawn than disruptive. They didn't fare well in large American public schools that had harried teachers and anonymous student bodies.

"I don't think this board really knows the meaning of alternative education," Ms. Henderson said. "When I first came here, we took high school students on field trips to Stone Mountain, but they didn't understand why we were doing that. They really don't know what alternative education is all about."

Clearly, she had an obstacle to overcome. She had to convince the board of education of the value of therapeutic as opposed to punitive alternative schooling. With her background in counseling, she naturally leaned toward more therapeutic measures.

The task was daunting. "I once gave a presentation before the board," Ms. Henderson told me, "and I knew it was hopeless when they wouldn't even look at me."

Therapeutic alternative educators preferred gentleness over harshness. They taught by example, praised often, and prided themselves on nontraditional classrooms. They maintained their tempers, were unfailingly polite, and did not retaliate against chronically disruptive students.

Punitive alternative educators, on the other hand, were more common, as evidenced by the preponderance of boot camps, scared straight, and tough love programs. Joe Clark, a much-lauded principal in the late 1980s, was well-known for raising test scores at the impoverished East Side High School in New Jersey. He also exemplified tough love by berating teachers, using a bull horn, and wielding a baseball bat. Clark appeared on the cover of *Time* magazine in 1988 and was depicted by actor Morgan Freeman in the popular film *Lean on Me*.

I knew that the general public was more supportive of punitive measures for chronically disruptive students than therapeutic ones. For one thing, adults were more familiar with punitive programs. If they'd heard of therapeutic alternative schooling at all, people often wondered, *Why reward bad kids?*

Ms. Henderson's task of edifying the school board was urgent because the board might close Peachtree Alternative at the end of the year. The school's academic counselor had received a phone call from the wife of a board member, giving her a heads up. Peachtree Alternative was in its tenth and, possibly, final year.

The signs were ominous. Neglect of the school buildings, dramatic staff cuts, and overcrowding pointed toward looming closure of Peachtree Alternative School. The fact that it had lasted almost ten years was amazing. It was a virtual dinosaur, as far as alternative schools went.

"I wrote the assistant superintendent," Ms. Henderson said, "asking her to please give me plenty of notice if they're going to close the school. I don't want my teachers to have to scramble for jobs at the last minute."

By this time, I was so interested in Peachtree Alternative School that I decided to stay and write a book. There were few books on alternative schooling and none on southern alternative schooling. I planned to explore the punitive–nonpunitive tension in a public school system and wondered if alternative schooling could succeed if the philosophical issue was not resolved.

Chapter 2

September

SEPTEMBER 3

Ms. Henderson had urged me to visit the academic counselor, so I sat on a sagging couch in the counselor's office. "You could write a whole book on this place in just one week," she told me. Her name was Ms. Wilkins. She had a kind face and wore standard teacher attire, a denim jumper.

The counselor told me she wore many hats. "I've been the school resource director, the link between the school and community," she said. "At one point, I wrote grants. I got a big grant to start a Boys and Girls Club in town, and it's still going strong. One year, we started a service learning project and built a park, right here in Franklin. It took a whole year. Kids rode dump trucks, backhoes, things like that."

Another environmental project, led by the counselor, involved a nearby wastewater treatment plant. Students helped collect samples of creek water and tested them for pollution. Both of the environmental projects showed students career options. The counselor had also taken students before a judge, not to be sentenced, but to learn what being a judge entailed. While at the courthouse, students also learned about the careers of bailiffs, court reporters, and lawyers. The counselor had arranged for other local business leaders, such as a golf shop owner and a restaurant owner, to speak to students about their careers.

In previous years, Ms. Wilkins had taken students to lobby legislators in Atlanta on behalf of alternative schooling. The activity helped teens develop communications skills. I spotted a photo of the counselor wearing a hard hat and rappelling equipment and learned that she and students had taken a ropes courses to develop leadership skills. During November, students

Figure 2.   The Side Entrance to the School.

even developed citizenship skills by doing something called Poll Patrol. They assisted voters, particularly senior citizens, to the polls. Students held umbrellas over voters' heads when it was raining as they entered and left the polls.

Speaking of umbrellas, the counselor said that she was one of the original founders of the school, and in the old days, the school building was in even worse condition. She used to have to sit with an umbrella propped over her computer to repel rainwater because the roof leaked so much. One teacher had as many as nine buckets in her classroom to collect rainwater. When a male teacher accidentally punctured a ceiling tile with his umbrella and the whole ceiling collapsed, the central office finally fixed the roof.

That year, Ms. Wilkins was not only the academic counselor, she was also acting assistant principal, at least unofficially, because the school no longer had one. She would be heavily involved in student discipline.

My next stop was Ms. Bates's high school English classroom. I found her reading *The Crucible* aloud. "Someone's here," a boy said. Ms. Bates waved, and the kids kept reading.

Half of Ms. Bates's classroom was filled with desks. The other half was divided into a reading center and a small computer center. The reading center had a couch, comfortable chairs, and a rack of magazines. Two stacked suitcases served as a makeshift coffee table. Ms. Bates's bookshelves held many young adult novels. I browsed the titles and spotted some of my favorites: the *Prydain Chronicles* by Lloyd Alexander, the fantasy books of Madeleine L'Engle, and historical novels by Christopher Paul Curtis.

The room was bright and eclectic. A large kite hung from the ceiling, ridden by a toy monkey. The couch had colorful throw pillows, and behind it, were shelves holding various art collections: vases, ceramic cats, and brightly painted miniature chairs. Ms. Bates had many photographs displayed around the room. In one, she hugged her two teenaged children. Another photo, from her days in Arkansas, showed her shaking hands with Governor Bill Clinton.

Several of the students were asleep at their desks, but Ms. Bates didn't wake them. In a college classroom or prep school, sleeping wouldn't be allowed, but things were different, here. When it was time for a sleeping student to read, Ms. Bates just shook him.

In some alternative schools, female teachers wore pants to deter sexual harassment. Some even wore sneakers so they could run. At Peachtree Alternative, however, Ms. Bates wore a pretty blue dress and heels.

"I'm tired of reading," a girl said about the play.

"I know," said Ms. Bates. "You have a long part, today. There's not much more."

One boy read his lines with dramatic flair. When the period ended, he slammed his book shut and declared, "I read the whole fucking thing!"

Just before school ended, the high school history teacher, Mr. Owens, invited me to his classroom, where I peered at his photos. One photo showed him on a family canoe trip. He also had photos of the submarine he had served on and mock battles that he had participated in as a Civil War reenactor. "The students like that I was in the navy," he said. Mr. Owens and I discussed the Tony Horwitz book, *Confederates in the Attic,* about Civil War reenacting taken to the extreme, and Mr. Owens was quick to say, "I'm not that hard core.

"How long are you going to be here?" he asked.

"All year," I told him.

"Well, good," said Mr. Owens. He was glad I wasn't going to be one of those visitors who swept in and swept out and then wrote something based on cursory observations. He headed out to bus duty then to graduate school at a distant university. He was taking extra courses so he could add a certification area to his teaching license. Ms. Bates was in graduate school, too, for a master's degree. At least she didn't have to drive far; hers was an online university. Not only were they alternative school teachers and parents, they were also graduate students. They both had a lot on their plates.

School was over, and the high school hall was eerily empty. I decided to check out a parallel hall, 200 Hall, which was for middle school and special education students. Special education students at Peachtree Alternative School were in self-contained, not integrated, classrooms.

On 200 Hall, I met more teachers who were decompressing together in a classroom. Ms. Henderson joined us, and we all perched in student desks. The teachers were friendly and invited me to visit their rooms. Mr. Martin, a new special education teacher, was the lone male on 200 Hall, and Ms. Singh, a tiny woman from India, taught a small class of special education students who were severely disruptive.

"Tell Ms. Hollowell about your students," Ms. Henderson told a middle school teacher.

The woman didn't hesitate. "Oh, they're awful," she said. "I love them, but they're awful."

A special ed. paraprofessional named Ms. Hackett was enthusiastic about a recent guest speaker. A naturalist from Sandy Bottom Nature Center had brought a hawk to school. "Next time, he'll bring snakes," she said then glanced at the principal for approval. "They're nonvenomous," she added. Ms. Henderson expressed concern about the snakes but didn't veto the visit.

Ms. Hackett had also brought a goat to stay at Peachtree Alternative. It lived in the enclosed grassy quadrangle in the middle of the school. Ms. Hackett thought it was good for students to experience caring for an animal. It taught them responsibility, helped them develop empathy, and paved the way for building relationships with others. I peered out the window and saw a small white goat tethered to a tree beside a pail of water.

"Her name is Trixie," Ms. Henderson told me. "Trixie is our school mascot."

"Does she get lonely out there?" I asked Ms. Hackett, which had occurred to her, too.

"I'm thinking of bringing in another one," she said and teased the principal. "If we have a fundraiser, will you kiss one of the goats?"

"I may pet it, but I won't kiss it," said Ms. Henderson.

Speaking of fundraisers, another special educator had a suggestion. She wore a black leather belt with metal studs that was at odds with her slender frame and long brown hair. She was the chair of the special education department at Peachtree Alternative School. "At my son's school in Tucker," the chair said, "the principal stood on the roof and did hula dances in a grass skirt. She also let students throw pie pans of shaving cream at her."

The idea did not appeal to Ms. Henderson. "You've got to remember our population," she said. "If our students threw pans of shaving cream at me, it would hurt. I've had to suspend eight kids, today, and did it alone because I don't have an assistant principal. I'm not very popular."

SEPTEMBER 5

"You missed all the excitement," a teacher told me at 8:15 on Friday morning. "It could have been a book in itself." Two boys had gotten into a fight at breakfast. (The cafeteria served two meals per day, and most students qualified for free breakfast and lunch.)

One boy had assaulted another and scraped his face, dislocated his shoulder, and tried to stomp on him. "I predicted William would blow," the principal said about the assailant. "I predicted it from day one, during orientation, when he sat with his feet on the table. When I told him to put them down, he said, 'You can't make me.'"

"Who stopped the fight?" I asked.

"Not me. I wouldn't get in there and break it up," said the principal, implying it was too dangerous. "The security officer pinned William down and cuffed him. We had to call an ambulance for the other boy."

I decided to observe special education and middle school, so I headed for 200 Hall. I passed a high school special ed. classroom and saw an Ashley Bryan illustration taped to a teacher's desk. Ashley Bryan was an award-winning children's illustrator who'd published more than thirty books. He was the winner of a Virginia Hamilton Award, a Coretta Scott King Award, and the Arbuthnot Prize for lifetime contributions to children's literature.

Ashley was also a family friend. My mother, a retired reading teacher, had met him when he visited her school, and they had been firm friends ever since. Ashley lived on an island in Maine but came to Georgia to visit his sister. I had one of his paintings in my living room and had even sponsored an exhibit of his handmade puppets when I worked at a children's museum. They were marvelous puppets made of driftwood, seashells, and beach glass.

I stopped to talk to the paraprofessional behind the desk, whose name was Ms. Pearl. She was holding down the fort until the special ed. department chair returned from an errand. "I found that in the library and really liked it," Ms. Pearl said about the Ashley Bryan picture. I told her about Ashley and said I'd try to bring him to the school the next time he was in town.

Ms. Pearl was very gentle with the older special education students. She had spent twenty years in the navy as a communications specialist before becoming a paraprofessional. "First, I was in San Diego then Pensacola," she told me. "I also lived in South America and Mexico. Naval bases were good places to raise kids. I have eight of them."

"Eight kids? Wow," I said.

"When we came back to Franklin, they didn't like it here. There's not much to do, but I wanted to be near family."

"Is this your hometown?"

"Right," said Ms. Pearl, "and a lot of my family still lives here. My parents and grandmother are here. I knew my great-grandmother, and I wanted my kids to know theirs.'

"Things have sure changed, around here," she said. "When I was growing up, there were a lot of dirt roads."

Ms. Pearl looked pensive. "There are so many pregnant teens, these days. I was young when I had my first kid, but at least, I was twenty. I've been married twenty-two years.

"Why don't you give Ms. Hollowell a tour of the room?" Ms. Pearl suggested to a boy, who led me in a wide circle. The fringes of the room were divided into centers. The reading center had young adult novels and comfortable chairs, the math center had board games, and the science center had a wall-mounted deer head that someone had donated. The boy lingered under the deer to tell me a hunting story.

I studied the daily schedule that was posted in front of the room. It was fast-paced, the exact opposite of high school block scheduling. Special education students wrote in their journals, read newspapers, and had math and language arts in quick succession. Lunch was followed by team work that took place outdoors, if it wasn't raining. An example of team work was relays. At the end of the day, special education students had an activity called "group." I understood that group was when they sat in a circle and reviewed their behavior.

My student guide led me over to a tall behavior chart that was taped to a wall. It was divided into zones. All students began in the lower zone and progressed upward. When a student's behavior improved dramatically, he reached the top of the chart, and it was time for him to return to regular school.

Removing students temporarily from mainstream schools and having them earn their way back was controversial. Many alternative school teachers doubted that troubled teens' problems could be solved in one semester. A common academic problem found in alternative schools was poor literacy skills, and correcting that took time.

Experienced alternative educators sometimes wondered if students should be returned to regular schools, at all. In some cases, regular schools contributed to problems by being too large to fulfill the needs of troubled teens, who needed smaller classes and more one-on-one attention.

"Do students want to go back to regular schools?" I asked Ms. Pearl, but my tour guide answered.

"Some do and some don't," he said.

I learned, later, that if Peachtree Alternative students opposed returning to regular schools, teachers sometimes wrote waivers for them to stay. In fact, some students had been at the school for several years, and some even graduated from the alternative school.

We headed to lunch. The cafeteria was freezing, and many students shivered in their shorts. In the South, old school buildings were often freezing in warm months and sweltering in the winter due to overactive air conditioning and heating.

I ate tacos with a retired school superintendent who was now volunteering at the school. He tutored students and sat in on classes when teachers needed a break. He was on familiar turf because he had once been a principal at Peachtree Alternative before becoming a superintendent.

Ms. Henderson dropped by our table. She asked the volunteer if he wouldn't mind looking in on a substitute teacher who was having trouble. I had spotted the substitute in the library earlier that day. He was elderly and had my utmost sympathy.

"It's been a stressful day," Ms. Henderson told us. "Fridays are always the worst."

She turned to me. "I have a title for your book," she said. "I think it should be called 'Thank God It's Monday.' Mondays are always better in alternative schools."

The volunteer explained. "It's because more kids are absent on Mondays, and the ones that are here are tired from partying all weekend."

"I'm exhausted by the end of the week," Ms. Henderson said. She suggested that I attend a disciplinary meeting she was holding. Five students had committed dress code violations. "There may be fireworks," she warned.

The principal passed by later, trailed by the high school history teacher, a parole officer, and five boys. We all went to the library, and Ms. Henderson directed the boys to some tables. They grinned as she scolded them for wearing baggy pants.

Each boy was called forward individually and told to lift his shirt. Three boys revealed pants that were hanging far below their boxers. Two others had added belts on the way over.

"Now, I'm giving you a second warning," said Ms. Henderson, "and if you come to school like this again, I'll cite you for failure to comply with the code of conduct. You'll go before a discipline committee. Peachtree County says you can't come to school like this."

One boy panicked and thought he was going to jail, but Ms. Henderson quickly reassured him, "It'll be a school hearing, not a legal proceeding."

The boys' parole officer, a handsome black man, spoke up. He told the boys they couldn't get jobs, dressed as they were. "Who's going to hire you with your pants falling off?" he asked.

Afterward, the adults had their own meeting. "The kids' attitudes are worse these days," the principal said. She mentioned an earlier incident when a girl started to walk right between her and a female parole officer while they were having a conversation.

"It was incredibly rude," said Ms. Henderson. "I pulled her back to stop her, and she said, 'Get your damn hand off me.'"

The principal shook her head. "I don't want to have to do this . . . discipline students for dress code violations. It's a waste of my time, but Peachtree County says I have to. Do you have any suggestions?" she asked us.

Some therapeutic alternative schools had eliminated dress codes altogether, but it wasn't an option in conservative, rural Peachtree County. No one had any suggestions, but the history teacher observed wryly, "Sometimes their pants even fall off."

One of the students who had just left was frustrating the history teacher in another way. "Justin won't even look at me," Mr. Owens said. "He talks constantly, and when I try to talk to him, he turns away. When I ask him in the hall if he can hear me, he says 'yes', but he can't focus. He needs Ritalin."

"I know," said the principal. "He asked me if he could please have his medicine, but the school can't afford it." She turned to me. "Last year, we'd give it to him first thing in the morning. Our nurse would hand it to him right away when he walked in the door, but he went off it this summer."

I knew that many parents stopped giving their children Ritalin in the summertime to give them a break from the medicine or to save money.

"I told his mother he needs more medicine," the principal said. "She made an appointment for him, but they never went." We sat in glum silence then went our ways.

I walked Mr. Owens back to history class and asked him more about his teaching. "Ms. Bates says I have a presence with kids," he told me, without conceit. "I don't know why. I just do."

I agreed, to myself, that the man had natural authority. He also had enthusiasm and compassion.

"I understand these kids because I used to be one of them," Mr. Owens said. "I used to have a white Mohawk and wear combat boots. Other kids used to beat me up. I didn't care about school and didn't want to graduate.

"Don't hesitate to give me advice. Ms. Bates and I are tight," he said, crossing his fingers, "but we're open to suggestions." I left Mr. Owens to discipline some loud students in the substitute teacher's room.

My day ended with a visit to the front office. The room was empty because the school no longer had a secretary, although a rare temp sometimes sat at the desk for a few hours. That afternoon, I walked directly into the principal's office.

Ms. Henderson filled me in on the opening days of school that I'd missed. The paramedics had come to school with their sirens wailing three times in August to treat a special education student with epilepsy. The paramedics found, while the student really did have epilepsy, he was just faking seizures.

The fourth time the student lay on the ground, the teachers could detect his eyes fluttering and suspected faking. The paraprofessional named Ms. Hackett stood over him and said she'd be scared to take him on field trips if he kept having attacks. The student popped up, and there had been no more episodes.

SEPTEMBER 12

"A substitute!" some kids yelled when they spotted me. Their tone was gleeful. A lot of kids enjoyed having a substitute teacher, which they interpreted as being able to goof off. Their bubble burst, though, when Mr. Owens walked into the room.

"You can sit at my desk," he told me and rolled out a new orthopedic office chair.

"Nice chair," I observed, and he agreed.

"Ms. Henderson didn't want me sitting in that other one." He pointed to a dingy, tilting chair in the corner.

There were twelve students in the high school history class, and only three of them were girls. Mr. Owens gave us all a handout. "This came off the Internet," he told me. "I also get stuff from an AP Web site. I don't want to dumb down the material."

Some of the kids did a measure of seatwork. Two boys were preparing to take the high school exit exam, and Mr. Owens had exit exam prep books for them. I browsed a dry prep book and pitied the kids for having to take exit exams.

Three kids slept and two read magazines while Mr. Owens taught those who were paying attention. It was triage education. He had to pick his battles, and keeping kids awake and constantly on task wasn't one of them.

Mr. Owens role modeled courtesy. He frequently said "sir," "ma'am," and "please." He also exuded calmness. "I never raise my voice," he told me later.

John Kellmayer, author of *How to Establish an Alternative School,* never raised his voice either. Kellmayer wrote that maintaining one's temper was vital in alternative schools. Alternative students were masters of confrontation, and if you engaged in an argument with them, students would invariably win. Also, Kellmayer thought that students would be more likely to turn to him in times of trouble if they could count on him to remain calm.

A boy named Mike, in a yellow tee shirt, stood out as a troublemaker. He whined and shouted until Mr. Owens took him into the hall. The rest of the students quieted down to listen and stared at the doorway. The pair returned, and Mike was quieter afterward.

Danita was a big, cheerful girl who kept taking swigs of grape juice from a clear jug with wads of chewing gum in the bottom. One boy sported a diamond earring, and I had trouble distinguishing between two girls who wore identical hairstyles and blue-jean miniskirts.

All three girls were tough. A miniskirted girl punched Mike in the arm while Mr. Owens had his back turned, and Danita told someone to "shut up" then looked sheepishly in the teacher's direction. Saying "shut up" was one of his pet peeves.

"Mr. Owens, are you leaving?" a boy asked.

"No, what makes you say that?"

"Well, she's here," the boy pointed at me.

"I'm not leaving," Mr. Owens assured him.

"We're getting a new teacher, though," the boy reported. "I was at a school board meeting, and they were deciding on an application."

"I don't think so," said Mr. Owens. "They must have been approving substitute teachers. No one wants to teach here." He was half joking, but the kids were immediately defensive.

"I ain't bad!" three kids said in unison.

"Of course not," said Mr. Owens. "Now, we're going to play a game." The class was divided in half to answer a series of questions. Each time they answered correctly, they'd earn a point, and the winning team could deduct the total number of points they earned from their next quiz. "I've given as many as seventeen extra points," said Mr. Owens.

The game didn't go well, though. The kids resisted and were lethargic. In fact, they were so unenthusiastic that Mr. Owens gave up. "I don't think I'm going to do this again," he announced.

"Fine, then don't. I don't care," said Danita, who clearly did.

Mr. Owens let it slide, and the ninety-minute period drew to a close. He moved to the back of the room and told me that he didn't like block scheduling. "I'm an adult, and it's hard to maintain *my* attention for ninety minutes. I'm taking graduate classes that are three hours long. We're wearing out toward the end there."

"What are you taking?" I asked him.

"Oh, just stuff for certification," he said, without elaborating. "I wanted to be a teacher so I could spend more time with my family. But I'm not spending more time with my family. If I'm not planning or grading papers, then I'm in graduate school."

"Did I hear your wife was a teacher, too?"

"She teaches at Holly Springs Elementary. She's been there fifteen years. Last year, she was teacher of the year there, and I was teacher of the year here. We were the first married couple to both be teacher of the year."

Ms. Bates came by with a list of names. On Fridays, students with good behavior could go with Mr. Owens to the gym to play basketball. Good behavior included not sleeping.

Some kids left the room, and others replaced them. A girl with blonde streaks sat in the desk beside me and began browsing a photo album. She wrote notes that she carefully shielded with a sheet of paper then practiced some calligraphy. Three kids slept in a corner. One boy slumped in a chair and propped his feet in another. He pulled his head, turtle-like, inside his shirt. Another boy hid beneath his sweatshirt hood.

A boy stuck out his tongue to show Mr. Owens the newly pierced tip. "Keep it in there," said the teacher. "If I don't see it, it's not breaking the rules."

Mr. Owens sat poised on a stool in the front of the room. Danita finished her juice, decided to participate, and answered most of Mr. Owens' questions. She wanted to know more about Thomas Jefferson. "I have a ruler with all of the presidents on it," she said. "What's so special about Thomas Jefferson?"

"Some people think he was a hero, but he did own slaves," Mr. Owens pointed out. "George Washington owned slaves, too." That was important information since many high school students still graduated not knowing that the two presidents had been slave owners.

James Loewen, who wrote *Lies My Teacher Told Me,* blamed whitewashed history textbooks for the widespread lack of knowledge about the Founding Fathers' misdeeds. He thought the authors of history textbooks were prone to hero worshipping and feared portraying the Founding Fathers in a bad light.

"Didn't George Washington chop down a cherry tree or something?" asked Danita.

"It's a myth that he chopped down a cherry tree then said, 'I cannot tell a lie,'" said Mr. Owens. "It's a story told to little kids to make them more honest."

Danita was indignant. "Then why do they tell us that in school?"

"My point," said Mr. Owens, "is not everything you're told in school is true. It's better to question and research things than accept them unconditionally. Remember what we learned about Columbus? He's considered a hero, but he did some bad things, like enslaving Indians."

Mr. Owens told Danita more about Thomas Jefferson. "He was a farmer and a politician and an architect who designed his own home. It was called Monticello, and it had a dome. Look at a nickel, and you can see it." Several kids pulled out nickels and examined them. "He was an inventor," Mr. Owens said and described some of Jefferson's inventions.

"He also slept with Sally Hemings," Danita pointed out.

"That's right," said Mr. Owens, "and he fathered many children."

"You must like history," I whispered to Danita.

"I do," she whispered back. Later, I learned that Danita was one of the students who was at the school, not for chronic disruption, but for falling behind academically. She had dropped out of school to give birth to twins.

"Do you have any questions?" Mr. Owens asked me as we headed for lunch.

"I wondered about the sleeping," I said.

Mr. Owens told me that one student in the last class was on medication that made him very sleepy. "I could go around rapping on desks all day or I can teach the kids who want to learn. We do have a reward system for kids who don't sleep.

"It's hard having eighteen kids in that class," Mr. Owens said. "I used to have five, and we could just sit at my desk and talk. It's a different bunch of kids this year."

Ms. Bates had a planning period after lunch, but she was going to tutor a small group of boys and said I was welcome to join them. "I'm going to teach 'Gilgamesh.' I haven't taught it before, so this ought to be interesting."

Three boys sat in the reading section of her room with lunch trays perched on their knees. Ms. Bates had brought food back from the cafeteria. She put the containers in a small refrigerator and explained, "I take extra food home for dinner."

Four more kids jostled into the room. "Mr. Wilson sent us over to cool off," said Danita. Mr. Wilson was the high school math teacher.

Ms. Bates sighed. "Okay," she said, "but I'm going to have to talk with him." I gathered that Mr. Wilson was using Ms. Bates as an *interclass suspension* officer. The school no longer had an in-school suspension officer so teachers had to come up with other options. Either they controlled their own kids or engaged in *intraclass suspension* (i.e., isolating students within their own classrooms.) An alternative consequence was *interclass suspension* (i.e., isolating students in someone else's classroom). *Interclass suspension* only worked, though, if the other class was filled with much younger or much older students.

"If you're here during my planning period," Ms. Bates told the additions, "the rule is you don't say anything." The extra kids sat at the computers and played games.

Ms. Bates ate apple crumble from a paper cup and studied her "Gilgamesh" notes. She handed me a printout. "I have to supplement the text with research of my own," she said. "Some of it's from the Internet. It takes a long time to find, and some of it's not so good."

"Gilgamesh" was a fun word to say, but the story didn't grab the boys. Only one kid responded to Ms. Bates's probes. She tried to elicit parallels between "Gilgamesh" and the Noah's Ark story but a lot of her questions hung in the air.

Students arrived for fourth period, and they weren't happy to learn they were going to have a test. Many alternative school students had a history of bad experiences with tests; therefore, some alternative schools, such as my friend's in Milwaukee, eliminated tests altogether, despite adult arguments that there were tests in the real world. At the Milwaukee alternative school, kids just compiled portfolios of their best work. Peachtree Alternative School was not that radical.

"How long is the test?" asked a student.

"Eight pages," said Ms. Bates.

"Eight pages!" whined several kids.

They had read *The Crucible* and had even seen the film version starring Wynona Rider. I thought that, surely, it wouldn't hurt them to buckle down. One boy tried to look at another's paper until Ms. Bates moved to a prominent position in front of the room. Most kids finished the test in under forty-five minutes and had free time until the end of the day. They read magazines, slept, or surfed the Internet.

Mr. Wilson, the math teacher, sent in yet another boy for interclass suspension. Mike, the boy in the yellow tee shirt, who had also been disruptive in Mr. Owens's class, flounced in. He flopped on a sofa and stewed and then pinched a girl's crotch when Ms. Bates wasn't looking. Mike bragged to another boy about waking up on the floor of his pickup truck clutching a whisky bottle and a .38 Special.

SEPTEMBER 15

A custodian spotted me. "You're here more than the regular teachers," she said.

The principal led me down the hall and introduced me to Ms. Cox, the middle school art teacher. She welcomed me into a colorful room. Bird mobiles hung from the ceiling. The walls were covered with papier-mâché masks and handmade ceramic tiles, and a life-size cardboard robot stood in a corner with its arms raised.

Ms. Cox was a striking woman with long, flowing blonde hair. She wore all black and sported a silver ring on every finger.

Four boys and four girls sat at tables around the room. One girl had an ugly black eye, and the white of her eye was bloody. Two plump girls named Heather and Brandy formed a gang of two in the middle of the room. Both girls wore round, wire-framed glasses. They threw out quips and mimicked Ms. Cox, but she ignored them. They especially liked to mimic Ms. Cox's enthusiastic tone as she gushed over students' artwork. She praised them generously. I thought that praise wasn't such a bad thing to echo. If you had to listen to something two or three times, why not have it be good? The alternative students might not receive much praise at home.

Ms. Cox also used frequent endearments. She called the kids "hon" and "honey" in a paradoxically gruff voice.

Heather and Brandy made a lot of unnecessary noise. They slammed their books shut and slapped their papers around. Brandy even banged on the table with the palm of her hand.

Despite their antics, I could see that they admired their teacher. The students had made collages, using images from magazines, and Heather's collage was all rings. She had glued pictures of different rings all over her construction paper. Ms. Cox's own ten rings glittered whenever she raised her hands.

The students moved from one activity to another, in quick succession. Ms. Cox was demonstrating successful teaching: being overprepared and keeping students busy with relevant projects. She avoided downtime.

The teacher showed me a CD. "I play symphonies," she said. "I have a bunch of them. I pop them in, and they're good background music. They're soothing."

Ms. Cox's organization was as good as her pacing. All of her boxes were clearly labeled. Laminated instructions for projects were posted all around the room, and computers were in a neat row with all of the screens visible. Large plastic cups were filled with sharpened pencils. A whole week's worth of assignments was written on the board.

The next activity was a drawing assignment. Kids were told to illustrate adjectives. They drew a total of twenty faces with expressions such as sad, angry, or scared. "I'm drawing you," Heather told Ms. Cox.

"Good," said Ms. Cox, in passing.

"I'm drawing her as funny," said Heather.

"How about crazy or stupid?" suggested Brandy.

Ms. Cox showed an art film. "Here's what they have to answer," she said, handing me a list of thought questions. "They're not just watching." The list of questions was long. Ms. Cox was challenging her students like Mr. Owens with his advanced placement materials and Ms. Bates with "Gilgamesh." They all had high expectations.

Ms. Cox sat beside me for a minute. "I try to give them plenty of choices," she said. "I like to have choices myself. I had some teachers that just bored me to death. You probably did, too. I give homework about three times a week and none on weekends, unless it's makeup work.

"I have a good storeroom and a kiln next door. I wrote a grant for it when I first got here. I don't have a sink, but we make do with a bucket."

She looked around the room. "These are good kids," she said, loudly enough for them to hear. "They're good kids. They just haven't made good choices."

"What's your story?" she asked me bluntly, and I told her about myself.

In turn, Ms. Cox said she'd been teaching for twenty-six years. Seven of them had been at Peachtree Alternative. We talked about ineffective punitive programs such as boot camps.

"I've been to boot camp," Heather piped up.

Ms. Cox nodded. "Heather's been here three years," she said. She pushed back her chair. "I don't know what I'm doing sitting down. I never sit down." Her regular circulating was another hallmark of good teaching.

"Remember to hand in your twenty faces," she told the kids. "That's your ticket out the door." She turned to me. "Come back any time."

I followed Heather and Brandy to their next class and introduced myself to Sara Woods-Jones, the physical education teacher, who had been forced to teach science at the last minute when the science position was frozen. I'd also heard that Ms. W-J, as she was called, was a champion weightlifter, so kids ought to think twice before messing with her.

We headed down 200 Hall, and it was a long, awkward walk. Some kids pushed, while others straggled. I had plenty of time to study the floor tiles, many of which were missing.

When we reached Ms. W-J's classroom at the end of the hall, it was obvious why she was wearing a thick woolen sweater. Her room was closest to the building's air-conditioning unit, and it was freezing. Some kids' lips were turning blue. They started shivering, and some clustered their chairs in a small patch of sunlight. Others put on jackets or just slipped their arms inside cotton tee shirts. Brandy wrapped herself in the one blanket in the room.

Ms. W-J opened all of the windows in an attempt to let in warm air, but that only increased the noise from the nearby air-conditioning unit. The rusted contraption absolutely roared. My own fingertips began to turn white.

Brandy called Heather a name. "*Excuse* me!" said Ms. W-J, who had super hearing. "That's not her name."

"It is, too," said Brandy. "It's Heather Honkey."

"I don't see that in my roll book," said Ms. W-J. I had noticed that Peachtree Alternative teachers were quick to admonish kids for racist remarks.

The kids watched a video on earthquakes then had free time. Two kids played a game of checkers while others talked quietly or drew pictures. It was a peaceful setting.

At 10:15, the room began to empty. "Is this a bathroom break?" I asked.

"We're going to lunch," Ms. W-J told me.

"So early?"

With the overcrowding and a relatively small lunchroom, lunches had to be widely staggered. Plus, preschoolers in a building, next door, used the lunchroom, too. Lunch began early and ended late.

Brandy shoved Heather, who was in front of her in line, and Ms. W-J shook her head. "These girls are something else," she said.

"They're pretty tough," I observed.

Ms. W-J corrected me. "They *think* they're tough."

Lunch was the three Cs: corn dogs, corn, and coleslaw. A visitor's plate cost $2.50. Ms. Henderson, who monitored the lunch periods, sat at a table just inside the door. Two round teachers' tables were placed near the cash register. The cafeteria staff had made them look nice with lacy tablecloths and plastic flower centerpieces. "No take out, today?" Ms. Henderson called to the teachers.

"No, we like corn dogs," a teacher said, waving hers in the air.

"It's quiet today," Ms. W-J observed.

"That's because Samantha has gone to prison," said another teacher.

Ms. W-J ate her lunch, quickly. "Time to go," she announced to her twenty students. "You need to wear a longer skirt," she whispered to a girl in a blue jean miniskirt.

We went back to the frigid classroom and had more free time. "Pull your shirt down," Ms. W-J told another girl, who was exposing her midriff. The girl pulled her shirt down, briefly.

Ms. W-J's final class was gym. She took students across the road to the gymnasium that was even more decrepit than the school building. Inside, the wooden bleachers were broken and the floor, beneath them, was littered with trash. Much of the paint was peeling from the walls, and a basketball hoop was missing a net.

All of the girls sat on the bleachers while most of the boys played basketball. Ms. W-J was the only female on the court until she sprained a finger.

The air inside the gym was stale, and the toilets didn't work. A frayed rope dangled from the ceiling, the scoreboards were broken, and a clock was missing. Some parallel bars listed in a corner. The gymnasium epitomized a neglected building and sent a strong message that the county didn't care about troubled teens.

SEPTEMBER 16

A community meeting took place in a large conference room across the hall from Mr. Owens' room. Normally, the conference room was locked, but today, it was filled with a dozen adults. The room smelled of coffee and biscuits, and tables were arranged in a large U shape.

The group was called Save Our Students (SOS). The director opened the meeting by saying, "We invite anyone who cares about children and youth in Peachtree County to participate." I sat beside Ms. Henderson, who identified others in the room. They included substance abuse counselors from a residential treatment facility, a deputy sheriff, and a nurse from a local health agency. The nurse was planning a health fair with blood pressure screenings and car seat safety checks. A local college professor, in charge of family literacy, was also in attendance. Her program provided picture books to new mothers in hospitals, encouraging them to read to babies. A foster father, who had several foster children in the school, sat directly across from me.

"Ms. Henderson, would you like to introduce your guest?" asked the director.

The principal stood up. "This is Mary Hollowell, and she's writing about our school. She's seen some very good teaching."

I agreed and told the group what I'd seen.

A substance abuse counselor added, "I work with a Peachtree Alternative students at the rehab center, and they love it here. They learn more here than they ever did at their old schools."

The foster father spoke next. "My son, Malcolm, goes here. He's the biggest kid in school."

"He certainly is," said Ms. Henderson.

"He wants to play varsity basketball but still go here," the man said. It was another testament to good teaching.

Ms. Henderson was still standing, and she rode the wave. "We have some good people helping us." She mentioned the former principal and superintendent, who was now volunteering.

She turned to the bad news. "We're hurting, though, because I've had to cut six staff positions." She named the losses. "We may even close."

"Now is the time to have some good PR," said a woman.

"Would it help if we wrote letters to the school board?" asked another.

"Absolutely," said Ms. Henderson.

After the meeting, the director approached the principal. "Is it really that bad?" she asked.

"We're going to be hit with more budget cuts in January," said Ms. Henderson. "That's going to affect everyone. I hear they may even cut paraprofessionals, although not in special education. They're talking about cutting programs, next, and we're one of them."

"What the board needs to realize," said the principal, "is this county is growing. We'll have more of these kids, and if they aren't in school with me, they'll be out on the streets. They'll be breaking into homes and starting fires.

"There's talk of putting the alternative students behind regular schools in trailers but that won't work," Ms. Henderson said.

I, myself, knew from reading *How to Establish an Alternative School* that nearby trailers wouldn't work because there would be mutual hostility between alternative and regular students. The two schools, in close proximity, would likely have two principals and two sets of rules, which would just be confusing. Over time, the alternative school would become more like the regular school with the anonymity that may have contributed to students' problems in the first place.

In *How to Establish an Alternative School,* John Kellmayer wrote that stand alone alternative schools were a better option than attached ones, although stand alone alternative schools in very remote areas bred violence. Remote alternative schools isolated students from society, and their students failed to interact with and learn from upstanding citizens. Peachtree Alternative School was somewhat isolated but not remote.

"There's some talk about building a new football stadium behind the high school," said Ms. Henderson. "We can either do that or educate these kids. We have to get our priorities straight."

After the meeting, I ran a guest speaker idea by Ms. Henderson. I suggested bringing author Ashley Bryan to visit, the next time he was in town, and she agreed.

"Where are you going, next?" she asked.

"To visit the new special ed. teacher."

"Mr. Martin?"

"He's invited me a couple of times, already," I said.

"Well, he's having some problems. Maybe you can give him some advice."

Seven boys and one girl were doing worksheets in Mr. Martin's special education classroom or, at least, they were sitting with worksheets in front of them. Two walls of the room were partitioned into cubicles. Each cubicle or cubby contained a desk facing the center of the room. Three boys sat in cubbies but the rest were at desks in the middle of the room. I didn't know what to make of the giant cubbies. Were they a prehistoric method of special education or a practical way to reduce distractions?

One student, who'd been especially disruptive, sat at a desk in the hall. Only two boys did any work. The rest just wandered around. They talked, shouted, and distracted their neighbors. Mr. Martin said "sit down" repeatedly but they ignored him.

Most of the students were in seventh or eighth grade. Only one boy, Matthew, was in the sixth grade. Matthew was at Peachtree Alternative for trying to strangle a teacher. I saw his eyes roll back once, and he shook his head to stop it. Later, I watched him suck his thumb. He was a dangerous adolescent and a toddler, in the same package.

Matthew watched me taking notes. "What are you doing?" he asked.

"I'm writing a book."

"We bad?" he asked because someone taking notes usually meant he was in trouble.

"You're not bad," I told him quickly, and caught Mr. Martin's eye.

I knew how important it was to combat negative labels. The history teacher and the art teacher had demonstrated that to me. Mr. Owens had quickly reassured defensive students that, of course, they weren't bad, and Ms. Cox had said loudly, "These are good kids. They just haven't made good choices."

Work time was followed by free time but both periods looked the same. Few of the kids could settle down long enough to focus on one project. Ms. Hackett, Mr. Martin's paraprofessional, returned to the room. She was the enthusiastic woman who had brought a goat to school.

A reading corner held a great set of books. I spotted Susan Cooper's fantasy *The Dark is Rising* and Jerry Spinelli's book *Maniac MaGee.* There were many good titles, and I itched to read aloud to the kids. I loved reading aloud.

There was so much movement going on. A big boy did nothing he was told to do and knocked over a can of soda on Ms. Hackett's desk. He did a poor job of cleaning it up. Basically, he threw all of her papers onto the floor and swabbed at a couple of sticky spots. He was the most disruptive kid in class. His pants were falling off, and he grabbed his crotch a lot. He stepped on Ms. Hackett's papers with big shoes that were unlaced.

The grownups in charge kept their cool. Matthew expressed an interest in the book, *The Hunchback of Notre Dame.* "Oh!" he said, grabbing a copy.

"You can read it, then watch the movie," Ms. Hackett told him. She pointed to a collection of videotapes lining a windowsill. "Then you can compare the book to the movie."

Ms. Hackett set Matthew up at a listening station. He and two other students listened to an audiotape of *The Hunchback of Notre Dame* and followed along in the book. They complained because the equipment was shoddy.

"I can't help it," Ms. Hackett said. "I have to buy it myself at garage sales because we don't have much money around here." Matthew listened longer than the other two kids. . . . a full five minutes.

"Remember to have your permission forms signed so you can go on the field trip," Ms. Hackett told the group.

"Where are you going?" I asked.

"Stone Mountain. We're going to the plantation because it fits with the Georgia history curriculum." I knew how important it was, in the era of accountability, to legitimize a field trip by carefully relating it to something the students were studying. There were no frivolous field trips. I suspected that Ms. Hackett was one of those highly creative educators who could make any subject relevant.

I asked to go on the field trip but said that I didn't want to take up space meant for children. "We have plenty of room," Ms. Hackett assured me. "We have a whole bus. The trip is for kids who've been on their best behavior. Some of them will stay here.

The students began lining up for lunch. "So," said Ms. Hackett, "could this class be a whole chapter in your book?"

"It could," I told her.

"You should stop by more often," Mr. Martin told me. "The kids were much better with you around."

I was surprised. *That was better?*

At the teachers' table, the paraprofessional named Ms. Pearl was struggling to shred her meat with two plastic forks. She explained to me that they didn't have plastic knives, anymore, because they could be used as weapons by dangerous children.

After lunch, I followed Ms. Pearl back to her room. It was raining heavily so the class stayed in during recreation time. Several boys played Monopoly. Malcolm, the biggest boy in the room, chose to work on a jigsaw puzzle with the smallest boy. Malcolm was at Peachtree Alternative for fighting in his regular high school. He had been one of only eight black students in a school of two thousand whites.

"Do you want to play a game?" a boy asked me. He was a tall black boy with red hair. I had watched the small teacher, Ms. Singh, shepherd him into the room with her hand on his elbow.

"What should we play?" I asked.

"You pick 'cause you're the grown up."

The boy's name was Jarrod. He'd been labeled MI for mental illness. I chose a nearby board game but couldn't find the rules. Next, Jarrod chose mancala but I couldn't remember how to play it. We settled on a jigsaw puzzle that was a map of the world and sat on the floor. The smelly carpet was ripped to shreds.

I pointed to Africa and asked Jarrod a teacherly question, "What continent is this?"

He didn't know, but he sure knew his Bible stories. He rambled on about David and Goliath and Daniel in the lion's den.

The special ed. department chair stopped by and patted Jarrod's dyed red hair. "Don't you like his hair?" she asked.

"It's a good color," I said.

The woman hugged Jarrod. "You have a good heart, son," she told him.

SEPTEMBER 24

I heard a radio crackle in the hall. "I need a resource officer immediately," the principal said. "Keep your students inside," she told Ms. W-J then shut the classroom door. We were in Lockdown Mode.

"What's going on?" a girl asked.

"I don't know. Just keep working," Ms. W-J said.

I started to imagine bad things. In a school where my mother taught in downtown Atlanta, a teacher was shot and killed by her estranged husband in front of her students. I thought about that, and I thought about Columbine.

The kids kept on working and didn't seem perturbed so they were faring better than the adults in the room. Ms. W-J went over to the door. "I wonder what's going on," she whispered to me. She cracked the door open and peeked out but didn't learn anything.

"We can't go until Ms. Henderson says we can," Ms. W-J told the kids and let them play games. Two boys squabbled over some blocks in a bin. "Quit being hateful," Ms. W-J said. "Can't we just love each other?"

She peeked out, again. "Can we change classes?" she asked someone in the hall, who said we could.

"Okay, you can go now," Ms. W-J told the students. "It's time for the restrooms."

Ms. Henderson sat in a chair at the far end of the hall. Some of the lights were out, and the end of the hall was dark. She was on guard. *For what, exactly?* It was a stark vision, the shadowy principal, sitting in the middle of the dark hall with her arms crossed. I wanted the scoop but she couldn't be bothered. Kids went to the restrooms, and I headed for the teachers' lounge but it was cordoned off by crime scene tape. I saw that the glass in the vending machine was shattered. A police officer hurried past me and headed for 200 Hall.

I had no choice but to use the girls' restroom, and it was worse than I had imagined. Only two of the six stalls had doors; the rest just had hinges. Only one stall had toilet paper. The seats slid around and were barely attached, and the room reeked of urine. The concrete wall beside the sink was crumbling, and overhead pipes were rusting.

Anxiety and depression began to weigh me down.

I rejoined the middle school students, and we filed back to science class. Ms. Henderson was now talking to the officer. I was last in line, and I heard her tell him, "This young man has cut his hand. You'll need to wear gloves."

Later, I learned the details of the lockdown, which was unrelated to the vandalism of the vending machine. On 200 Hall, a special education student had gone on a rampage. He was in a time-out room, alone with the chair of special education, and he went ballistic. He overturned tables, threw chairs, and broke windows. The chair, who was considered to be a calm woman and an excellent educator, said it was the first time in all her years of teaching that she'd ever really been afraid.

The student started threatening to commit suicide. The counselor arrived and was able to calm him down. They sat on the floor until help arrived.

The boy was from a broken home and his mother was an alcoholic. After the rampage, teachers found out that, the week before, the student had broken a beer bottle and used it to cut up his little brother's face. The doctor had to put in so many stitches that he lost count. Afterwards, shockingly, the little brother was returned to the home.

Ms. Henderson said that the student was volatile and had no business being at the school. Removing him would be difficult, though, because she must first prove his violent outburst was not a manifestation of his disability. Many authorities would be involved in making the decision: special educators, school administrators, police officers, psychologists, and social workers.

Chapter 3

October

OCTOBER 7

I sat in computer class and listened to students squabble. "Tell this kid to get off my computer before I hit him," a boy told the teacher.

"He has to download something. He'll be done in a minute," the teacher said. The boy struggled to maintain his composure while another kid leaned over him and tapped on the keys.

There were only two girls in the room and one of them was very large. A boy beside her kept smart-mouthing the teacher. "Nelson, come in the hall," the computer teacher said but the kid didn't budge. The teacher repeated himself, and the boy rose slowly.

"I don't want to go see that lady," the student said about Ms. Henderson, who was an effective deterrent to student misbehavior. "No way. She got me in trouble, last week." The computer teacher escorted him to the principal's office, anyway.

A couple of boys napped in front of their computers while a third boy, named Deshawn, said to the teacher's departing back, "I ain't scared of you. Nothing scares me. I've seen someone shot point blank in the face. I'm from the hood." He sang a dirty ditty, and the girls giggled.

The computer teacher came back, and a girl asked if she could borrow his cell phone to call her father. "You know I can't let you do that," he said. "It's against my policy. If I let one student use my phone there'd be a stampede."

"Then can I go to the office to call my father?" the girl asked.

"Later," said the teacher.

"When?"

"Just later!" the teacher snapped.

Figure 3. A Horse-Drawn Paddy Wagon from a Field Trip.

Deshawn was distracting some girls, and they were having a boisterous conversation about parties. "Deshawn, I want to talk to you to see if we can improve your mouth and your work performance." The teacher took him into the hall and gave him a lecture. We heard him use the word "respect" a few times. When they returned, Deshawn worked quietly at a computer and was better behaved for the rest of the period.

The computer teacher praised the kids who had been busy working. When the student returned from the principal's office, the teacher told him, "Tomorrow is a new day. We'll start fresh," and I admired the man's clean slate approach.

School ended, and the computer teacher and I walked to a faculty meeting. "I had kids in there, today, who were back at school after being suspended for five days," he told me. "That was part of the problem. Was it as hard to watch as it was to teach?"

"It's never as hard to watch as it is to teach," I told him.

The faculty meeting was held in Mr. Owens' room, and Ms. Henderson had us arrange our chairs in a circle. "Just help me put them back," Mr. Owens said. The tired teachers formed a makeshift circle.

Ms. Henderson told the group that she had asked for plenty of lead time, if the school closed, so they could look for new jobs. No one said a word in response to the solemn news.

The counselor tried to point out that the recent budget cuts didn't just impact Peachtree Alternative School. "They were across the board so it's not just us," she said. Ms. Wilkins was a born cheerleader but her words didn't help matters.

"Remember to donate your vintage items for our school fundraiser," the principal told the teachers. "Ms. Hackett is collecting them." She also reminded teachers that they had parent conferences coming up in two weeks.

"I've already met with parents," a teacher said. "Do I have to do it again?"

"You can't meet with parents too many times," said Ms. Henderson. She emphasized the importance of teachers contacting parents at home, early on, with positive information so they set a good basis for future conversations.

Ms. Henderson scolded the teachers, briefly. "Be on time. Some people are not on time. That doesn't mean checking your mailboxes or getting coffee. It means being in your rooms and on duty."

Ms. Bates, as chair of the alternative high school, handed out a mandatory questionnaire that teachers had to complete then mail to central office. Teachers complained, and one of them said, "They're just going to get carried across a marble floor and sit on a mahogany desk." She was referring to the fact that the central office was located in a brand-new, four-million-dollar office building that was full of frills. The expensive decor stung when you were understaffed and surrounded by squalor.

The alternative teachers received their supply stipends for the year. Each of them got $350, except for the computer teacher, who got $500 to repair computers. At Holly Springs High School, ten miles away, supply stipends were $1000 each.

With the money in hand, the counselor suggested that Peachtree Alternative teachers buy cakes for the regular schools and attach thank you notes. "It's something sweet to do for them, and it's good PR," she said. Ms. Wilkins reminded teachers that regular schools were filtering students to them and they were filtering them back.

"They ought to be buying us cakes," a teacher mumbled.

OCTOBER 9

I'd read in Greg Goodman's *Alternatives in Education* that The Talking Heads' "Road to Nowhere" was a good field trip theme song so I listened to it on my way to school. I was going to be a chaperone, and teachers met in the cafeteria.

The special education teachers had dressed casually for the field trip to Stone Mountain. Mr. Martin was wearing jeans. Ms. Hackett was wearing a polo shirt, and Ms. Pearl had on a plaid flannel shirt. We all wore comfortable shoes.

Only a few kids were allowed to go on the field trip. One girl had to stay behind because she forged a note from her mother, and the rest had just been too rowdy.

Ms. Hackett and I carried drinks and sack lunches to the curb and waited for the bus. The driver and I loaded the coolers. "Are these special ed. students?" he asked me, and I nodded. "I used to drive a special ed. route," the man said, and when the kids started coming, he knew them. "Tom, my man!" the driver said to a small boy, and the two shook hands. "Pete, you've grown," he told a white boy who was wearing a purple bandana on his head. I had only seen Pete wear purple and black to school. He was originally from the Bronx, and those were his gang colors.

Only seven students climbed on board the bus. It was a small group, indeed. There were twelve of us, altogether, including the driver, but we had a bus that seated forty. Ms. Pearl, Mr. Martin, Ms. Hackett, and I were the four chaperones, and the odds were in our favor.

Jarrod with the dyed red hair sat beside me and rested his head on my shoulder. His hair was smelly but I didn't push him away. "Jarrod, get back here!" Ms. Pearl yelled from the middle of the bus. She pointed to a seat across from her, and Jarrod moved. The driver gave a safety speech, and we headed out.

Ms. Hackett and I sat up front, and she told me about her own children. She was the mother of three. Her youngest child was twelve and her oldest was seventeen. They attended Holly Springs middle and high schools. Ms. Hackett pointed out the schools as we passed them.

She was a big fan of thrift stores and showed me some good ones along the way. It was part of the reason she enjoyed the school's vintage shop fundraiser, so much.

Stone Mountain, the largest free-standing granite rock in the world, loomed before us. A quirk of Stone Mountain was the giant carving on the face of the mountain. The carving showed three mounted Confederates in profile: Stonewall Jackson, Robert E. Lee, and Jefferson Davis. The bas-relief sculpture was nine stories tall and covered an area of three acres. The detail that I remembered most from childhood was that sculptors ate lunch up there on the brim of a hat. None of the students on the bus could name any of the figures so their assignment was to find out who the men were.

First, we visited the quarry. "Can we walk by ourselves?" Pete asked Ms. Hackett, who was clearly the leader of the expedition.

"Yes," she said, "but don't get more than fifteen feet ahead of us. And pull up your pants." Pete's pants were about to fall off, and Ms. Hackett used a clever ruse to induce cooperation. "I don't want your pants dragging on the ground and slowing me down," she said.

Pete's small posse sped away and the rest of us followed. The adults took a few minutes to read interpretive signs. Some historical photographs showed the giant sculpture under construction.

We wandered over to a grist mill. "What was this used for?" Ms. Hackett asked the students.

"For making wishes," said Jarrod, staring into the water.

"I mean what was it used for, long ago?" asked Ms. Hackett. None of the kids knew.

Jarrod was confused. "It is *so* used for making wishes. Look at all the pennies." He turned to me. "Isn't it used for making wishes?"

"*Now* it is, but she means in the 1800s."

"Get away from the water!" Ms. Hackett yelled at Tom, who was about to fall into a lake. He and Pete were holding some tackle boxes that they'd found beside a rock. "Put those back," Ms. Hackett yelled. "They have hooks in them. If you took hooks to school, they'd be considered weapons."

The boys set down the tackle boxes. Pete lost interest, but Tom popped one open. He slipped some hooks into his pocket and started tossing others into the water. Ms. Hackett didn't notice immediately, and I hoped that no one waded in barefoot.

"Tom, what are you doing?" Ms. Hackett called. "Stop that!"

"Are they still in your pocket?" I asked Tom about the hooks. Ms. Hackett made him turn his pockets inside out but the hooks were gone, and I felt a powerful headache coming on.

We reboarded the bus and waited as Purple Pete stood outside and downed a can of cola that he couldn't bring on board. Next, we headed for Old Town. It was a quaint area of country stores, glass blowing and blacksmithing shops, and a theater featuring a film on swamps.

"Pick an adult," Ms. Hackett told the kids, and they all picked me. Undoubtedly, I was the most naïve adult, which accounted for my popularity. Ms. Hackett made most of them take Ms. Pearl, instead. She asked me to keep an eye on Jarrod while she bought our tickets. Mr. Martin was in charge of big Malcolm and little Matthew, the strangler. The bus driver followed us all into Old Town.

I had no problem keeping track of Jarrod, who literally hung on my elbow, but the rest of the kids fanned out. The other teachers watched them wander off, instead of calling them back. Old Town was crowded on a sunny Friday afternoon and was filled with tourists and school groups. Ms. Hackett grew exasperated and grumbled, "They need to keep track of those kids." She told me that her worst fear was losing a student so I started counting heads at regular intervals, and my head really began throbbing.

I needed to change a twenty dollar bill so I wandered into a candle shop looking for something cheap. I bought a smelly candle in the shape of a Georgia peach for fifty cents. Jarrod started pestering me to buy him something.

"If I buy you something, everyone else will want something, too," I said. I tried to distract him by steering him towards the blacksmithing shop but he warned me that the smoke would trigger his asthma.

Instead, we went into a Christmas shop with a candy counter and, naturally, Jarrod wanted some. "Buy me this," he said, holding up a giant lollypop. I saw Mr. Martin give Tom some money and my resolve began to crumble.

I compromised by buying myself some cheap candy, eating a piece, and giving the rest to Jarrod. That way, I wasn't exactly violating my own policy.

Jarrod ate candy, and we wandered out into the sunshine. He bent over and grabbed his head. "Oh, my eyes hurt," he said, and I started to panic, thinking maybe he was diabetic and not supposed to have sweets.

Jarrod groaned, and Ms. Hackett hurried over. "Come in the shade, Jarrod," she said. "Sit in a rocking chair." Jarrod and I both sat. He groaned some more and Ms. Hackett told him, "If you get sick, I won't be able to take you on any more field trips." Jarrod recovered instantly, and I remembered that he was the boy who faked four seizures at the beginning of the school year.

Ms. Hackett spotted an old fashioned paddy wagon with metal bars that was a prop for pictures. At first, none of the alternative students would go near it. "I ain't going to jail," Tom said. The kids had a strong aversion to the paddy wagon, even though it wasn't real. Finally, Kim, the only girl in the bunch, and then Jarrod, were persuaded to climb in. They rattled the bars, grinned, and had their pictures taken.

We managed to round up the kids and go inside something called a 4-D theater that was cool and dim. We collected 3-D glasses from bins at the entrance. Banjoes played through hidden speakers as we waited in line. Crickets chirped and frogs croaked. A larger school group was in front of us in the lobby, and we were towards the back. Some innocent bystanders were squashed between us. They turned out to be employees from a telephone company. Their leader started a conversation with Ms. Hackett, who was excited to learn that they were looking for mentoring opportunities. The two women exchanged phone numbers.

Doors swung open automatically and we were swept into a movie theater. Fake branches, draped with Spanish moss, hung overhead. We all sat in a row and donned our 3-D glasses, and the film began.

The main characters, a boy and a girl with thick Southern drawls, paddled into a swamp in search of their grandfather. The special effects were dazzling, although the plot was thin. A snake slithered out from the screen and opened its jaws, and kids in the audience screamed at its dripping fangs.

The snake spat venom while, simultaneously, drops of water fell on us from somewhere overhead.

"This is scary," Jarrod whispered, but he was smiling.

I tested the screen without my glasses on. It was all a big blur. The movie wasn't helping my headache, and I didn't have any aspirin.

The kids onscreen peered into a hollow tree and bats flew out. Air was blown on to us to simulate the bats fluttering past. A giant Sasquatch-type creature pounded through the swamp, and our seats vibrated.

The grand finale was a thunderstorm. Lights flashed overhead, wind blew, and we were sprinkled with more water. We headed outside and blinked in the sunshine. Ms. Hackett tried to get the kids to watch a glass blowing demonstration but they weren't interested. Purple Pete wandered off to talk on his cell phone, and Jarrod spotted some cute teenaged girls. He grabbed the bus driver's arm. "Call them over," he said about the girls.

The driver played along. "I can't. I have a wife," he said.

There wasn't time for us to view a giant map of Georgia, made of flowers, so we climbed back on the bus and headed for the plantation. I wondered how accurate the plantation tour would be and if there would be any discussion of slavery. Sometimes, they glossed over slavery at antebellum tourist traps.

No one was available to give us a guided tour, though, which bothered Ms. Hackett. She had worked hard to plan a fun and educational field trip. The ticket taker explained that they had recently cut back on costumed interpreters because of the small number of visitors. We set off on our own, and the only employees we saw were a couple of guys hauling off dead tree limbs from a recent thunderstorm.

Both the smokehouse and historic kitchen were empty. "This field trip sucks," said Kim. We peered into the schoolhouse then mounted the steps of the mansion only to discover that it was locked. That really upset Ms. Hackett who stormed off to get our money back. The barnyard had Vietnamese pot-bellied pigs, which were historically inaccurate.

We were running late so the kids would have to eat their sack lunches on the bus rather than under the towering oak trees. "Buses have to be back by 1:30 so they can start the afternoon routes," Ms. Hackett explained. She had managed to get at least some of our money back.

We sat in our regular seats, and Big Malcolm began to complain. "I'm going to tell my mama this was a bad field trip."

The whining spread, and another boy said, "I'm going to tell mine, too."

"Fine, tell your mothers," said Ms. Hackett, whose feelings were hurt. She looked at me and said loudly, "I didn't see anyone having a bad time in the theater, did you?" I said that I didn't, and the kids stopped complaining and fell asleep.

"So what did you think about their behavior?" Ms. Hackett asked me.

I admitted that I really didn't know much about special education. "I can see you need a lot of adults, though, because they wander off. Is it because they're easily distracted?" I asked, and Ms. Hackett nodded.

"I was hoping Ms. Wilkins would come along so we'd have someone with authority," said Ms. Hackett. "I was disappointed in Pete's behavior and in Tom's."

"I think you did a good job running the show," I told her.

Having to be in charge alone, though, had worn Ms. Hackett out. Paraprofessionals were paid a pittance, and she did the work of a teacher. I wished that I could have been more helpful. "You have dark circles under your eyes," a kid told her.

"It's probably low iron. Do I have dark circles?" she asked me. It was a question along the lines of "Do I look fat?" that I avoided answering.

"Well, your cheeks are pink," I told her. "I think you've gotten some sun." I hoped she had good plans for the weekend. She deserved some rest and recreation. I, myself, was ready to down some aspirin.

OCTOBER 16

The day came when I was asked to be a substitute teacher. Ms. Henderson and the teachers had so generously let me observe in their classrooms that I felt I owed it to them to substitute. I was vaguely worried that I'd be too popular, since the pool of substitute teachers was very limited. After all, Ms. Henderson had told me, "I can't get substitute teachers to come to this school."

I was fortunate that my first substitute teaching was in special education so I wouldn't be in there alone. Ms. Hackett was out, that day, so I would be replacing her as a paraprofessional. I'd heard from Ms. Henderson that Ms. Hackett liked me, and the feeling was mutual. I wanted to help the woman out.

The sun was just beginning to rise when I arrived at the school at 7:30. Mr. Owens walked out and signaled a bus driver to let the high school kids into the building.

I waited in the cafeteria with some other teachers. "Smile, it's not so bad," the counselor told a girl but she wouldn't smile. She had been in a fist fight, recently. Her grades were poor, and I heard her tell other students, "I don't care if I fail. I'll just go out and sell drugs."

When a teacher told me that the special education students were better behaved than the regular kids in the building, she jinxed me.

"You're supposed to wait in the classroom," Ms. Henderson told me. "Your kids don't come in here, right away."

I went to Mr. Martin's room but the lights were off and the door was locked. The chair of special education suggested that I go wait outside for the buses with a paraprofessional. A small boy was keeping the parapro company. When I told her who I was subbing for, she said, "Oh, you poor thing," and gave me a hug.

Ms. Cox, the middle school art teacher, hurried past the blue dumpster in front of the building, clasping some books. She wore a black shirt and black tights under a denim jumper. *Those jumpers sure were popular with teachers.* The paraprofessional gave her a big hug, too, and Ms. Cox beamed. "I needed that," she told us.

Two school buses arrived, and the alternative special ed. students stepped out. They didn't pour out eagerly, but that probably doesn't happen at any school. The students clutched their books and moved slowly, looking sleepy. Jarrod wore a white woolen cap, and his eyes were hooded.

"Good morning, Jarrod," I said, but he barely noticed me. He was so withdrawn that I wondered if he was being bullied on the bus. Bus stops and school buses were prime spots for harassment, and he was a vulnerable kid. Cameras and ride along adults were known to curtail bullying on buses, but I didn't see those measures on board.

I followed the special education students to the cafeteria, for breakfast, and waited in line with the other teachers. Mr. Martin told me that two boys in the class had court dates coming up. Matthew, who tried to strangle a teacher, would go to court, next week. Another small boy named Leon brought a knife to school and threatened to cut off a student's finger. I wondered what was keeping him from bringing a knife to Peachtree Alternative. The school had no cameras or metal detectors and only one regular security officer.

Mr. Martin said the lecture method didn't work well with his kids. "At least, it doesn't work for me," he said. "Maybe it's because I haven't been here very long. They're better with one-on-one instruction and I give them worksheets." Worksheets sounded an alarm with me, because they always struck me as busywork.

"How are they with being read to?" I asked. "I like reading aloud."

"You can try it," he said. "I have an article I want them to read. It's about Zheng He, a fourteenth-century Chinese explorer."

I'd been thinking more along the lines of reading aloud from a great chapter book, not some article of Mr. Martin's. But it was his class, and I was the one who brought up the subject. I felt compelled to read his article.

Mr. Martin took advantage of my agreeableness by asking me to substitute some more, next month. "That's fine," I told him. He teased me during breakfast. "I'm going to leave you in there by yourself," he said.

"Don't do that," said Ms. Pearl.

"No way. That would be cruel," said another teacher.

Ms. Henderson went over to the special education students and lectured them about their inappropriate clothing. "You cannot wear pants that fall off," she told them then came over to the teachers. "Who is that boy in the purple bandana whose pants are falling off?"

"That's Pete," said Mr. Martin.

Ms. Henderson was surprised. "That's our student of the week?" she said and shook her head.

Mr. Martin went and got his Zheng He article and handed it to me during breakfast. "It's from *Cricket*," he said, and I was pleasantly surprised. *Cricket* was a very good children's magazine. I skimmed the article. I liked the story and would do an impromptu lesson, even though impromptu was not my style.

Back in Mr. Martin's room, I demonstrated that I knew the students' names. I went around and named all eight boys. It was a popular trick in my old college classrooms, but it alarmed the alternative students.

"How do you know my name?" one asked, suspiciously.

First, the boys did journaling. They were supposed to write five sentences. Tom wrote about his plans to go fishing and another boy wrote about how much he hated writing.

Some boys were slower than others. "Do you want a prompt?" I asked a boy but he didn't understand. I rephrased the question. "Do you want me to give you something to write about?" He nodded. "Okay, why don't you write about football?" I suggested, and he did.

Leon, the sixth grader who threatened to cut off someone's finger, drew pictures and finally eked out two sentences. The boys read their journals aloud, and Mr. Martin gave them all As, even though they mumbled practically every word. The boys mumbled badly. Between that, their slang, and their thick southern dialects, I had a hard time understanding them.

"You're on," Mr. Martin told me so I began my impromptu lesson on Zheng He. I wrote his name on the board. I told the boys about his journey from China to Kenya in the fourteenth century.

"I'm interested in China," I told them, "because I'm going there to adopt a little girl." The personal information just slipped out of me but no one blinked.

The students and I looked at a globe, and I had every boy trace the route from China to Kenya. I told them details, such as most of Zheng He's sailors were criminals so he had a hard time preventing mutiny. One of the maps that he used was twenty-one feet long, and he kept a band of musicians on board to keep the fleet together during foggy weather.

"What else do we know about China? What was invented there?" I asked and gave the boys hints. "What do we shoot in the sky on the fourth of July?"

"Fireworks," Tom shouted.

I mimed pushing a wheelbarrow.

"Wheelbarrows," said another boy.

"What do you put your feet in when you're riding a horse?"

"Stirrups," Tom shouted.

"And the Great Wall," added Leon. When I finished my impromptu lesson, he surprised me by leading a round of applause.

"Why, thank you, sir," I told him.

Afterwards, the boys had free time. Some of them gathered around the classroom's one computer while others watched a Three Musketeers video. "I try not to show them too many videos," Mr. Martin said, "but everyone else around here does it."

Ms. Henderson had warned me that Mr. Martin was having problems in his room. Between worksheets and excuses, his teaching was beginning to concern me. I didn't see a lot of effort on his part, and on the field trip, where he was the only real teacher, he had failed to take charge. His paraprofessional had run the whole show. Granted, Mr. Martin was new but he should have stepped up to the plate. Kids, even alternative special education students, could sense who worked hard and who didn't, and they acted accordingly. Elbow grease showed. Mr. Martin wasn't applying it.

"How do you think it went?" he asked me about my lesson.

"It was too short. It was probably a whopping fifteen minutes. You're going to have to go over Zheng He, again." I noticed that Mr. Martin had extra copies of the article on his desk so maybe he was going to do something in depth. That, at least, was a good sign.

"I really meant for them to read the article," Mr. Martin said. "I'd like for them to read more. If I could only do two things, it would be to have them read and do math. I want them to hold down jobs, once they graduate." The man's heart was in the right place. I asked him more about himself. He had attended a local university, and his teaching certificate was in social studies, not special education.

A boy wanted to switch the movie to *George of the Jungle,* and an argument ensued. Things did not bode well when Mr. Martin told me, "Free time is the most dangerous time around here."

Free time turned out to be chaos, especially when Mr. Martin stepped out. The boys chased and punched each other, and it was hardly a big room, just eighteen by twenty feet. Mr. Martin came back and yelled, "Sit down. Sit down," but it didn't do any good. I thought that the boys probably shouldn't have any free time at all. They should have nonstop structured activities.

My paraprofessional friend, from that morning, stopped by to help maintain order, and I was thrilled to have another adult in the room. "How are you doing?" she whispered, and I must have looked stricken because she gave me another big hug.

Jarrod had joined us, and I thought that, at least, I could help Jarrod. He was the gentlest boy in the whole school. He showed me two toys that he had in his pockets, two plastic action figures. Leon pestered Jarrod to hand them over and when he did, Leon started beating the figures together.

Lunch couldn't come soon enough. I sat beside the academic counselor and ate my hot dog and chips. She had something to show me, an essay she had written about a recent bad day. On that particular day, there had been a suicide threat, an assault on a teacher, a drug bust, and several brawls. Still, Ms. Wilkins was optimistic about the future. She thought that at least four of the seven board members would vote to keep Peachtree Alternative School open.

The principal dropped by our table and asked me, "Are you ready to come every day?"

"Nooo!" I groaned then was embarrassed. I had applied to be a teacher, after all. There I was admitting that I couldn't even handle four hours. I had forgotten that I was speaking to the principal.

"Ms. Hollowell, I appreciate your honesty," the principal said.

The counselor raved about the baked beans so I tried a few bites. Over at the special education table, Purple Pete had no lunch at all. *How could he get through the day on an empty stomach?* "Why isn't Pete eating?" I asked his teacher, Ms. Singh.

"Pete never eats here. He doesn't like the food," she said.

One thing in Peachtree Alternative's favor was its well-run cafeteria, thanks to an experienced cafeteria manager named Betty. The kitchen usually received perfect scores on health inspections, except for a time or two when a light bulb was out. Obtaining a perfect score was no easy task in a kitchen filled with old appliances.

After I ate, I interviewed Betty, the cafeteria manager. "Our dishwasher went down so we have to wash all the dishes by hand," she told me. "When inspectors come, the water has to be a certain temperature. I'm on pins and needles about the temperature and have to change the water every ten minutes." The washing machine was broken, too. "I'm washing towels at home in order to have clean towels." I thought Betty's having to use her own machine was uncalled for.

She and her cooks were proud of their meals. "My staff and I cook like we'd cook at home. We use seasoning and add variety." It was frustrating for Betty, though, when she fixed good food and kids didn't eat it.

The lunchroom staff made a special effort for the teachers by giving them extra dessert. During holidays, they even decorated the cafeteria walls. It was Betty's fourth year at Peachtree Alternative School and her twentieth in food service management. She knew most of the alternative students by name, which was hard because they were always coming and going. New students flooded into the school, each week, while others left for youth detention centers. "It's hard to keep up with the flip flop," Betty said.

After lunch, the special education teachers decided which students would have more free time, based on their behavior. The good kids got to go to the gymnasium. I headed to the gym with Ms. Singh and some of the better-behaved boys. The tiny woman carried a huge bag of battered basketballs, which I offered to help carry.

We went down a back hallway that I hadn't seen before. It was abandoned and was nicknamed The Derelict Hall. The lights were out and many ceiling tiles were missing. A long row of doors led to classrooms that were only used for storage. I jiggled a handle, and it was locked.

The view from the windows of the Derelict Hall into the enclosed, grassy quad was depressing. The rusted gutters and boarded-up windows were clearly visible. We exited through a side door, and the boys ran ahead of Ms. Singh, who yelled in vain for them to stop.

Jarrod offered me his elbow, like a gentleman, and we walked that way over to the gym. The building was as decrepit as I remembered.

Jarrod called me over to play basketball, and I joined his group. I shot baskets with him, Leon, and Ms. Singh but when some bigger boys came in, I ducked out of the game and sat down to watch.

A bigger kid swiped the ball from Jarrod and Leon, and the pair gravitated in my direction. They sat beside me on the bleachers, and Leon pestered Jarrod for his action figures, which were in his jacket pocket. Leon made a few grabs.

"No!" Jarrod said and yanked his jacket away. I began to notice that Leon cackled a lot, and it was disturbing. Many students at Peachtree Alternative School were victims of physical and emotional abuse, as well as poverty, and I had to remind myself that Leon was probably a victim.

"Would you tell him to leave me alone?" Jarrod asked. I saw Ms. Singh watching us from across the gym, waiting to see what I would do. Tom kept flipping the gym lights on and off and plunging us into pitch darkness, which didn't help matters.

"Give me your jacket. I'll keep it with my things," I told Jarrod. He passed it over, and I waited to see if Leon would try to grab it. He was focused on the toys and seemed oblivious to my presence, which made me think he might also be autistic. I'd be better able to cope if I knew what the students' various disabilities were. I *knew* what their crimes were. A lot of the boys probably had ADHD.

Instead of grabbing the jacket, Leon grabbed Jarrod's cherished and tattered astronomy book that he'd also brought from home. It would be a miracle if Jarrod managed to keep his personal items. I wasn't going to allow snatching so I tried to take the book back but Leon just ran away, cackling. He slung the book across the floor. I retrieved it, and Ms. Singh announced that it was time to go.

By that time, Tom, the kid who'd stolen fishhooks, was in a corner of the gym, hiding behind an old leather vault. He had found some paint and a brush and was covering the wall with graffiti. I began to lose my cool.

Back in our room, Mr. Martin tried to give a math test. I wondered if that was wise, considering it was Friday afternoon and we'd just had free time. The students fussed about the test but took it. Later, Mr. Martin showed me that most of them had just filled in random answers.

Leon had yet to do any work. "He's worried about going to jail," Mr. Martin told me.

We had more free time and more chaos. Mr. Martin left me and the friendly parapro, while he did whatever it was he had to do. I thought the man disappeared too often. A preschool teacher from the building, next door, stopped by and fussed at us for letting a boy escape. "Is this your student?" she asked, holding Tom by the collar. I hadn't even noticed he was gone.

The parapro was not going to claim Tom. "Well, he's Mr. Martin's," she said.

The preschool teacher reproached us. "You need to keep him in the room. He's not supposed to be bothering preschoolers," she said, and I was ashamed.

Three boys settled down to watch a DVD on a laptop computer they'd borrowed from a teacher. They watched a segment of *The Fast and the Furious* in which a man threw gasoline on a car then lit it. It was a dreadful thing for them to watch. They wanted to replay the flaming car scene but I confiscated the laptop. The boys promptly began punching each other until the department chair stopped by. "That is not respectful behavior!" she told them. "You apologize to Miss Mary."

"I'm sorry," they said.

The department chair pulled me aside. "You need to watch Leon," she said. "He's been making threats, today. Let me know if he does it, again."

"Will you come with me to get some water?" Tom asked. He was not supposed to go places, alone, but he followed that rule selectively. I escorted Tom around the corner to the water fountain, and he kept jumping up and knocking ceiling tiles askew.

Back in the classroom, he began playing a verbal sparring game with another student. They insulted each others' mothers. "Your mama is so old," said Tom, "that when the Red Sea parted, she was sitting there fishing." The other boy shot back with an insult of his own.

"Hello, Miss June," the paraprofessional greeted the custodian when she came to empty the trash can. I looked around the room and absorbed the terrible mess. The boys had has overturned chairs, dropped balls of paper on the floor, and thrown writing utensils. It was a complete disaster area. "Is it always this messy?" I asked the custodian.

"This must be a shock to you," she said, sympathetically, and I nodded. "They do make them clean up before they go," she told me.

The boys began ragging on each others' clothes. I knew they were just playing but when they started in on physical attributes, the game had to end. One boy told another that he had buck teeth and a big nose.

Mr. Martin returned and it was time to clean up the room. The boys made a cursory attempt to straighten things. Mr. Martin had overheard the last few insults. He sat the boys down and gave them a lecture on bad behavior. "You've thrown things and been disrespectful," he told them.

"I know you want to go back to your home schools," Mr. Martin said, but I wasn't sure that was the case. "Who wants to go back?" Mr. Martin asked and only two boys of the eight boys raised their hands. "Well, if you want to go back, you'll have to straighten up," he said, and I thought he needed to come up with a better incentive.

Finally, Mr. Martin dismissed the students for the weekend. His car was in the shop and he lived near me so I gave him a ride home. Mr. Martin was kind enough to thank me for substituting. "You did a good job, today," he said.

"Well, maybe I made a modicum of difference," I responded. My self-esteem was shot by then. I had simply been a baby-sitter for a bunch of boys.

"I thought your lesson went pretty well, today," Mr. Martin said.

"Thanks," I replied, grouchily, "It was all of fifteen minutes."

"I almost quit, awhile ago," Mr. Martin said. "If I'd been offered another job, I would have taken it. Things are better, now.

"You have to remember these kids have it rough," he said, telling me what I already knew. "They've been kicked out of integrated classrooms, then self-contained classrooms, then sent to Peachtree Alternative. They have no confidence. Some of them don't try so they won't fail."

"I know," I told him. "I know they have hard lives."

We were tired and not really following each other. I thought about The Derelict Hall and the crumbling gymnasium. "It's such an awful building," I said.

"Well, most alternative school buildings are bad."

"That's true," I said. We pulled up to his house. I wanted to be more helpful so I asked, "Is there anything you'd like me to prepare for Monday?" I was subbing then, as well.

"Not unless you want to try something new. I like to watch other people teach." He stepped out of the car.

"Let me look through my lessons," I said through the window. "Maybe I can find something interesting."

"Remember, if you do something with these kids, you have to keep it up. They don't like change, and they don't like new people," said Mr. Martin.

Then why didn't you just say "no" to my offer? I turned huffy. He and I were not on the same page. "In that case, I won't plan anything. That's easier on me." I drove away.

Later, I realized I really would have to plan something in order to combat the chaos. I packed a large book bag with a funny children's book, Richard Peck's *A Long Way from Chicago,* some markers, and designs for the boys to color. They could color while I read aloud. My mother, a retired reading teacher, always had kids color while she read aloud, even older ones. She just made sure the designs were sophisticated.

I was determined to be a better substitute teacher on Monday.

OCTOBER 19

Monday morning, as I was dressing, I removed the brooch from the lapel of my blazer. It occurred to me that with its long pin, it could be used as a weapon.

When I arrived at the school for substitute teaching, Mr. Martin was in his room talking on the phone to a parent. He was talking to a father about his son's misbehavior so I stepped into the hall to give them privacy. Ironically, at that very moment, the boy in question was starting a fight with another student.

The fight began in another room and spilled into the hall in front of me. The slender department chair tried to intervene and was caught in the middle. A boy threw a heavy metal trashcan and it bounced off her back and rolled down the hall. He was aiming for the other student but the woman was in the way. Tiny Ms. Singh stood in a doorway shouting, and I ran to get Mr. Martin. He pulled both of the boy's arms behind his back and escorted him, forcefully, to a time-out room.

I was appalled that a teacher had been hit by a trashcan, but she shook it off quickly. A security officer came and went into the time-out room, while the department chair filled out a suspension form.

The rest of us went to breakfast, and I was temporarily put in charge of a new boy named Derrick. He was at Peachtree Alternative last spring, but returned to his regular school in the fall. He didn't last at Holly Springs Middle School for very long, though.

Derrick's speech was slow and stilted. Almost proudly, he told me he was caught on a field trip with a dozen cigarette lighters. *Great,* I thought, *an arsonist.*

He showed me where, last year, he punched a locker. The gray metal had a large dent. Derrick hugged a teacher who was walking past then told me, "Last year, I said I'd kill her."

"It looks like she's forgiven you," was all I could manage.

The boy told me he was getting a migraine, and I thought it was a shame that the school no longer had a full-time nurse.

I sat at the teachers' table and ate a pancake breakfast. "Derrick Wilson is back," Ms. Pearl announced to the other teachers, speaking of the arsonist.

"Oh, no!" a parapro said, ominously. She wasn't feeling well, that morning, but when I suggested she go home, she said, "No, I'm in charge of ISS, today."

What I had been calling the time-out room was officially known as ISS or In-School Suspension. The special education staff had to take turns manning ISS, themselves, since the building no longer had an in-school suspension officer.

"Who's in there, today?" asked Ms. Pearl.

"Melody is in there, all week," said the parapro.

"Oh, you poor thing," said Ms. Pearl. I looked around for Melody, one of only three girls in special education, and saw her huddled in a patchwork quilt that she must have brought from home. Melody didn't look difficult, at the moment.

The department chair joined us at our table. I asked if her back hurt from the trashcan, but she said she was fine and that the kid who'd thrown the trashcan just needed medicine. "It's a shame when they can't afford it," she told us. "It's too expensive, and I don't blame parents for not wanting to pay eighty bucks a bottle."

I marveled that she could be hit with a heavy metal trashcan and still sympathize with the boy who did it. The woman was a real trooper. She'd even bounced back quickly from last month's rampage, when a student threw chairs and punched out windows. Why, the very next day, she was telling us how hard students' home lives were. Many alternative students had indeed experienced traumas.

Back in our classroom, I counted heads. With two kids suspended for fighting, we were down to six boys. "This is going to be an easy day," Mr. Martin told me.

The boys started writing in their journals, except for the new boy and Leon. Leon sat beside a box of newspapers and started pulling them out and throwing them on the floor, just like a toddler. Derrick, the new boy, refused to do any work so I didn't press him.

Derrick started yelling at another boy for no apparent reason. The other boy was all the way across the room. Insults flew through the air. "So you think you're a bad ass, huh?" Derrick shouted. "I can take you!" It honestly reminded me of my parents' Yorkshire Terrier that was always barking at much bigger dogs.

Derrick's mental illness was becoming more and more apparent, and the two boys rose to duke it out.

"Settle down," Mr. Martin said, with a hand on Derrick's shoulder.

"He started it," the other boy retorted.

"I don't care. Just get to work," said Mr. Martin, and Derrick called me over. He had decided to do some work, after all. He had difficulty reading and spelling but we finished the exercise. A kid beside us helped out by suggesting some sentences for Derrick to transcribe.

The boys gave oral reports, and their next task was a geography crossword puzzle. It was a smash hit. I hadn't seen them so interested in schoolwork before. They shouted out suggestions for 2 DOWN and 4 ACROSS, and Mr. Martin confirmed their answers.

My one-on-one instruction with Derrick was so successful that I tried it out with Leon. He also let me help him and we worked on the crossword puzzle, together.

Even free time wasn't so bad, that morning. The boys liked the film, *Harriet the Spy,* even though the star was a girl. They liked it because it was familiar. The film was set in a school, where Harriet was bullied and sought revenge by pulling pranks on fellow students. Later, she learned that revenge was not that satisfying. It was quite a good story.

Derrick sat beside me. "My shoes hurt," he whispered and slipped them off. He propped his feet, in gray socks, on the table.

I didn't have a problem with it. It was a far more minor infraction than throwing a metal trashcan at a teacher. The kid was just watching a movie. Why not let him be comfortable? His feet didn't even smell.

Tom complained, though, and Mr. Martin battled to have Derrick put his shoes back on. Derrick complied but also stood up and started banging his head against the wall, over and over again. I was horrified.

At lunch, I told Ms. Pearl about the head banging. "It was pretty alarming," I said, which was an understatement.

Ms. Pearl had taught Derrick, last year, and she tried to reassure me, "He doesn't do it hard enough to hurt himself."

I was thrilled to learn the department chair was coming to the gymnasium with us. Maybe she could halt the havoc. "What should we do in there?" she asked the other teachers. "Should we juggle? I still have those juggling pins in the closet." The teachers agreed that juggling pins might be hazardous.

It was time to go before Ms. Pearl even finished her lunch. She groaned and dropped her half-eaten sandwich. "I wish we had more time. Did you know that special educators are the only ones who don't have a planning period?" she asked me.

We went down The Derelict Hall, and the department chair and kids headed out the side door. I locked the door behind them and exited out the front.

The department chair organized a free throw competition by dividing us into two teams. I had to play in order to even out the teams and managed to make a basket.

Unlike the other teachers, the department chair constantly circulated around the gym. This kept brawling to a minimum. When she left Ms. Singh and me alone, though, behavior began to deteriorate. I was a coward and felt safer sitting on a bench beside Ms. Singh than in the thick of things.

Matthew, the strangler, started wrestling. One boy lobbed a ball at another, and Ms. Singh yelled in vain for them to stop. That afternoon, Purple Pete was the one who kept switching off the gym lights, leaving us in darkness.

"Have you ever been hit?" I asked Ms. Singh.

"What do you mean?"

I thought it was a pretty straightforward question, and it was a distinct possibility with that crowd. I rephrased it. "You've never been hit by a student, have you?" She gave me a strange look and didn't answer. Just then, I was hit in the face with a football.

"Are you okay?" a boy had the grace to ask.

"I'm fine," I said, rubbing my nose.

A renowned troublemaker from another classroom wore blue boxers and his blue jeans were falling off. He decided to take a break from shooting hoops and sexually harassed Ms. Singh. He played with his cell phone. "Look, it says, 'fuck me'." He showed her a text message. "Fuck me," he repeated, gleefully.

Ms. Singh scooted away from him and he laughed. He soon lost interest in the phone and, when he put it down, Ms. Singh took it.

On the other side of me, Derrick kept saying he felt sick and needed to call his uncle to pick him up. I'd already sent him to the temporary, part-time nurse, and she couldn't find anything wrong. She thought he was faking. There wasn't much more I could do. I tried to cajole him into hanging on a bit longer. School was almost over.

Ms. Singh had unlocked the front door of the gym and laid the heavy padlock on the bench. Derrick picked it up and began to play with it. In and out, in and out, in and out, he plunged the key, and he appeared to be fixated. I watched him plunge the key and felt more and more unsafe. I imagined him whacking me on the head with the heavy lock. The students were unpredictable so I went with my instinct and put more space between us. All of the brawling that I'd seen, lately, was getting to me.

On the way back down Derelict Hall, a kid huddled in a corner beside a water fountain. His back was to the hall and a stream of liquid was shooting out behind the fountain. *He was urinating in the hall! It was the last straw!*

"Leave that fountain alone!" shouted Ms. Singh, and the kid released a pipe. He had been fiddling with a pipe behind the fountain and just pretending to urinate.

"I fooled you!" he shouted at me and burst into laughter. He and another boy exchanged high fives.

Back in our room, our group was supposed to be reading a chapter from a textbook and answering thought questions, at the end. It was not a compelling activity, and when Mr. Martin stepped out of the room, some boys started arguing. One boy raised a chair overhead to smash another boy.

I leapt into action and distracted them with a book from my substitute teacher kit that I'd packed as a precaution. I pulled out an urban legends book that I thought would appeal to teenaged boys. I quickly announced that I was going to read urban legends and they must tell me if they thought the stories were true or false. The boy with the chair lowered it, and everyone sat down.

"This first one is about a mouse in a bottle," I said. "Have you heard of it?" A few boys had.

"I don't care about a mouse in a bottle," said Tom. "Don't tell me about a mouse in a bottle." He pulled his hood over his head but the other kids were listening.

I ignored Tom and read the paragraph. "Do you think this story is true?" I asked. Some boys did and some didn't. "Well, it's true," I told them and explained the story's origins.

"The thing about urban legends is people always say they're true. They also say a friend of a friend told them the story." We went through some more urban legends such as the alligator in the sewer and the spider in the hairdo. I had screened all of the legends, beforehand, to make sure they were appropriate. Mr. Martin came back and laughed at the last one, and I told myself that it wasn't such an off-the-wall lesson since Halloween was just around the corner.

Derrick pestered Mr. Martin to let him use the classroom phone. "Can I please call my uncle?" he whined. Mr. Martin caved, and Derrick had a loud conversation with his uncle. "Will you come pick me up?" he asked but his uncle refused. Still, Derrick said, "I love you," at the end of the conversation. That touched me, but I was also surprised that Derrick said it in a room full of boys.

Mr. Martin announced more free time, then promptly left the room. Derrick started to stand on a table. I whipped out some designs from my handy book bag. I grabbed some markers and plopped them on a table, and Derrick sat down.

The first story that I read from *A Long Way from Chicago* was about a man named Shotgun Cheatham. The name was fun for me to say and I thought that, surely, a humorous story about guns and a dead body would appeal to the group.

My efforts paid off and at least some of the boys colored while I read aloud. The other half of the room played computer games. Derrick and Leon colored at my table, and some others did mazes that I had brought. I managed to create a safe zone, and it was a tranquil half hour. To a visitor, the boys might even have appeared studious.

By the time I'd finished reading the entire first chapter, it was time for them to go. "I like what you did with them, today" Mr. Martin said. "I probably should have had more planned for them."

"Bye, Leon," I said to the last boy leaving the room and wondered if he'd even respond.

"Bye," he called from far down the hall.

Chapter 4

November

NOVEMBER 4

On 100 Hall, Mr. Owens was looking forward to teaching Civil War history, using a trunk filled with artifacts. "Even some adults don't know the colors of Yankee and Confederate uniforms," he told me, as he began setting up. He hung uniforms on coat hangers all around the room. Two boys watched but most students paid no attention at all. Mr. Owens hung a bed roll and canteen to the left of the board and an assortment of jackets, to the right. He told the class that soldiers in the Army of Northern Virginia wore dark gray jackets, which was confusing in smoky battle conditions. He placed a pair of muddy boots on the table in front.

Mike, who had bragged about his .38 Special, wandered around the room as Mr. Owens was setting up. "My mama's boyfriend used to reenact at Stone Mountain," he told the teacher.

"That's not reenactment. That's living history," said Mr. Owens but Mike didn't ask about the difference.

Mr. Owens pulled a wide-brimmed hat from his trunk. "This looks like a preacher's hat," he told us. "My wife likes it. It used to be stiff but, over the years, it's started to droop. It's seen too many campfires and too much sleet." I thought that despite his denials, if Mr. Owens sat in the sleet, he was probably a hardcore reenactor. He held up another hat, a floppy brown one, and crushed it to demonstrate its softness. "Ten years of reenacting have done this one in."

A pair of pants had patches and suspenders. "These are my first Civil War pants," Mr. Owens said, proudly. "My grandmother made them from an original costume." He held them up to the light. "You can just about see through the wool, it's so thin."

Figure 4.   Word Written in Blood Inside a Solitary Confinement Cell.

The math teacher, from next door, stopped by to look at the clothes. He spied a pair of pants made from thick wool. "Try wearing that in the heat," Mr. Owens told him.

The math teacher whistled. "Kind of rough, isn't it?"

"In hot weather, they're insufferable." Mr. Owens pointed to another uniform. "I marched in that coat in 104 degree weather." *No, indeed,* I decided, *Mr. Owens did not take Civil War reenacting lightly.*

Mr. Owens did not make students take traditional, multiple choice history tests. "I'm bombarding them with information," he said. "It's too hard for them to remember everything." Instead, he had them do projects and give presentations. Students chose an area of the Civil War that they wanted to focus on.

"Danita and Sugar are doing women in the Civil War," Mr. Owens told me. Danita was the mother of twins, and Sugar was a tiny black girl whose ponytail was sprayed hot pink. Her pink belt said "Hot Babe," and pink thong underwear showed when she bent over. "Do you want to do civilian women?" Mr. Owens asked them.

"What's a civilian?" asked Sugar.

"It's women who weren't in the military. Some women disguised themselves as soldiers. One soldier turned out to be a woman when she was wounded in battle and they ripped open her jacket." The girls listened with interest. "Another woman was discovered when she was in a prisoner of war camp."

"What happened to her?" asked Danita.

"Nothing. They just sent her home."

"We'll do women soldiers," Danita said, quickly.

Some students wouldn't quiet down until Mr. Owens told them, "I was up late, last night, packing this stuff. I'm sharing personal things with you, and I deserve respect."

He held up a biography of a boy named Eli, a Confederate soldier. "He was about your age," Mr. Owens said. "He was just sixteen. This book is based on a packet of his letters that was found in the street."

He held up other items as he described conditions in camps and talked about weather and disease. "The mud was shoe-mouth deep. Do you know what that means?" He raised his muddy boots. "It means it was deep enough to the cover the top of a boot and get down inside.

"This is state-of-the-art 1860s footwear. They're 'straight last,' which means they can be worn on either foot. The rough part of the leather is on the outside for waterproofing but I can tell you that it doesn't make a difference. The times I've worn these and it's rained, I've been soaked through, pretty quickly.

"There's no traction on these." He showed us the slippery soles. "If you were walking with a bayonet and you slipped on a patch of pine straw, you'd be in big trouble." If Mr. Owens could get permission from the school superintendent, he'd bring a bayonet and musket to show the class. "We'll go through how you fire a musket. I like to have students handle it because it's heavy. It really gives you a sense of how hard it was to be a Civil War soldier."

Mr. Owens was being the kind of radical teacher that Martin Haberman, author of *Star Teachers of Children in Poverty,* would approve of. He was willing to fight for a special project because he knew it would enhance learning. Demonstrating weapons in a class filled with alternative students who'd been labeled "dangerous" and "disruptive" was radical, indeed.

Last year, Mr. Owens didn't receive many signed permission forms from parents saying their children could view a weapons demonstration. The poor response was more due to student apathy than parental reluctance. Students just forgot to give parents the forms. So this year, Mr. Owens planned to use the opposite tactic, ask for a signature if a parent *didn't want* her child viewing a weapons demonstration.

Mr. Owens hoisted a frying pan, and I regretted that I didn't have my camera handy. "This would hold 'a mess,' a meal for about ten people," he explained.

A boy in back had eyelashes that must have been the envy of many girls. He slouched low between two chairs. His neck rested on the back of one chair, while his feet rested on the seat of another. "Put on an outfit," he told Mr. Owens, then snickered.

"No," said Mr. Owens. "If you'd been here in previous years, you would have seen me wear one. I've done it before. It's not funny. It's just a uniform."

He did, however, don a coat for us. "It sure has a lot of buttons," said the boy with long lashes who, despite his slouching, was paying attention.

"Soldiers usually just buttoned the top button," Mr. Owens said. "You can look at old photos of men sitting in front of the Franklin courthouse, and you can tell who was a Civil War veteran by the way they buttoned their coats."

"A soldier would get his uniform and go off and see the world," Mr. Owens said, marching back and forth in front.

"Then he'd catch cold and die," said Mr. Eyelashes, wryly.

We learned that one of a soldier's most critical items was his canteen. "But something would happen," the teacher said. He swept his finger inside the mouth of the canteen and held it up.

"Rust," said Mr. Eyelashes.

"Right, but you'd get used to it."

One of Mr. Eyelashes's neighbors asked how soldiers kept their water cool. "They didn't," said the teacher. "Not in the hot sun but they didn't care.

It could be boiling hot and they'd still want to drink it—that's how thirsty they were."

Ms. Wilkins passed by and saw the artifacts. "How cool," she said. I noticed that the back of the classroom door was hollow and had two big holes punched in it.

Mr. Owens picked up a haversack. "This rests on your left fanny. They're not very comfortable and weigh a ton. Your knife and fork and maybe a newspaper that you took from some Yankee would be in there, too." A few boys were watching with their mouths wide open, listening intently.

Thick squares of hardtack crackers were passed around the room. "A baby could teethe on that, all day long, and never make a dent but it softened up in coffee." Students leaned over each others' shoulders to study the crackers, and Mr. Owens only got better. He raised a tin cup. "All meals were eaten in this."

"And you drank from that, too," said Mr. Eyelashes.

A big knife got everyone's immediate attention. "I have cut myself on this knife so many times," said Mr. Owens. "Sometimes, I reached in my haversack and grabbed it accidentally."

He passed around some Confederate money. "Is this real?" asked Danita, fingering the bills.

"It's counterfeit," said Mr. Owens. "My brother and I made it but I can bring in originals." Not surprisingly, the counterfeit money really grabbed the alternative students' attention, and they wanted to know how to make it themselves. "With a scanner," said Mr. Owens, building on their interests, deviant as they might be. "Union counterfeiters would make up notes and flood the South with counterfeit money so that a barrel of flour would really be expensive."

He moved on to another topic that interested alternative students . . . bullets. He slipped a leather cartridge box over his head. "A company here in Franklin, Georgia, made the straps for Confederate cartridge boxes." Mr. Owens passed around some actual bullets from the 1860s. We all handled various bullets and listened to the different types of wounds they inflicted.

"That's a very rare bullet, right there," Mr. Owens said, pointing to one making the rounds. "It has a star on the bottom. That's the manufacturer's emblem."

"How much did you pay for it?" asked Sugar. "A hundred dollars?" She was surprised to learn that her teacher only paid a dollar for a Civil War bullet at a roadside stand.

Mr. Owens patted his canvas haversack. "In case you're wondering, guys, not all of this stuff on the outside is dirt. Some of it is makeup from a movie I was in."

Students, naturally, wanted to know what movie and he told them *Andersonville.* "Were you a star?" asked Mr. Eyelashes.

"An extra," said Mr. Owens. "Last year, I offered fifty points to any student who could find me in the movie. I knew all the scenes I was in but couldn't ever find myself. If it was in wide screen, you would have seen me but, on TV, I was cut off. Last year, a student finally found me."

"That was a really interesting class," I told Mr. Owens, afterwards.

"I used to visit elementary schools with my trunk," he said. "It's nice to be able to use it in my own class. I also bring in World War II uniforms. I wish I had uniforms from all the wars."

"I had a doctor come visit my class, once, when I was in the second grade, and he passed around a brain. I remember holding that brain in my hands." He pointed to his Civil War gear. "If I can use this stuff to help students remember something then I'll be happy."

NOVEMBER 14

Ms. W-J was replacing a teacher who went to a tribunal. The teacher had tried to break up a fight and ended up being punched in the mouth. The students, in the other teacher's classroom, had been assigned some math problems but the volume rose steadily. "Talking needs to stop," Ms. W-J said from the teacher's desk, up front. A couple of boys tossed a pen back and forth across the room, and a kid slammed a dictionary shut a few times. "I don't need any noise," Ms. W-J told him, and he stopped.

"Leroy, be quiet," she told an enormous kid who was talking loudly to a buddy. She told him only once, and Leroy hushed. The alternative students were prone to delaying, but Ms. W-J was eliciting quick responses that indicated their respect for her as a teacher.

"Close your mouth," Ms. W-J told another boy, and when he did, she thanked him. Ms. W-J issued orders firmly, with courtesy, and only once. Students surprised me, further, by lining up quietly to have her check their answers.

Two boys battled by writing insults on dry erase boards and flashing them at each other. The game impressed me because it was quiet and had a writing component. "I'm going to get you, Leroy," a boy flashed. He erased his board then wrote some more. "The same thing I done to Pee-Wee, if I have to."

Leroy grinned and wrote back, "Boy, stop." I doubted that many kids actually messed with Leroy because he was so huge.

"I've got to go to poll patrol," a boy told Ms. W-J.

"Don't tell me. Ask me."

The boy got into the spirit of writing on dry erase boards by flashing a request at his teacher. His board read, "May I go be a good citizen?" and Ms. W-J excused him.

She caught a kid drawing a cartoon character on a desk and made him wipe it off. As we changed classes, she whispered to me, "It's getting rough, around here." As winter approached, regular teachers were sending more and more students to Peachtree Alternative School. I had even heard that stalwart Ms. Bates had cried, one afternoon, when a student threw a book at her.

I followed Ms. W-J into her own classroom for second period science. Heather and her buddy, Brandy, spotted me. "Hi!" Heather shouted.

"Hi, Heather," I said, which sent her into a fit of giggles because she didn't know I knew her name.

Ms. W-J distributed an earthquake word search of her own design. It was called a "bent and wiggly" because the hidden words weren't just vertical and horizontal. The kids spent a good thirty minutes working in small groups to find the answers.

"Can we go backwards?" asked a small, cherubic-looking boy who was at Peachtree Alternative for bringing a knife to school.

"No, you can't," said Ms. W-J.

Just like the geography crossword puzzle in Mr. Martin's special education class, the science word search was a big hit, and I made a mental note to stock up on word games for my substitute teaching kit.

During lunch, Ms. W-J told me, "We may not be here, next year." The uncertainty was weighing heavily on her.

"I've heard," I said, "but it sounds like most board members are on your side."

"That won't matter if there's a budget crunch," she said with certainty. "Board members vote differently when it comes to money. There are supposed to be big cuts in January."

The art teacher joined us at the lunch table. Ms. Cox ate in silence, although she did say, "We have too many students." I asked how large her classes were and she said, "Seventeen in one and sixteen in the other, and we're supposed to have a maximum of fifteen." I sympathized with her because she had, by far, the smallest room of all the teachers. Some of it was even filled with art supplies so she had to be cramped.

"Ms. Wilkins told the board about our overcrowding but they don't care," said Ms. Cox. "I'll bet they'd care if we all walked out."

Some better-behaved students lined up for the vending machines and came back loaded down with sugar: candy bars and bottles of pop. There was not a single healthy snack or diet drink among them. The worst-looking combination was a boy's licorice sticks and neon green soda.

As we headed back to 200 Hall, a boy's baggy jeans fell to his ankles but he hiked them up without missing a beat.

NOVEMBER 17

Ms. Bates's high school English class was an oasis of peace, in the mornings, which helped compose many students who arrived from chaotic households. Students may have been physically or verbally abused, at home, but in Ms. Bates's class, they could relax and listen to classical music. The smell of baking bread even wafted through the windows from the kitchen, next door.

Ms. Bates gave students a cheerful "hello." Friday was blue jeans day for teachers, and she wore jeans and a green sweatshirt. She bustled around, gathering materials.

Ms. Henderson made announcements over the intercom and named the student of the week, a girl in our class. A couple of kids congratulated the girl and she ducked her head shyly. I'd never seen her before. In fact, there were many new kids in the building. The entire student population at Peachtree Alternative was exploding.

Ms. Bates handed a progress report to another new girl, who demonstrated her disdain by balling up the report. She tossed it into the trash can but Ms. Bates ignored her.

Ignoring student misbehavior, if it was minor, was a very useful technique. "Differential attention" was its technical term. I had seen Ms. Bates and Ms. Cox use "differential attention" with good results. Some things just washed right over them. Ignoring misbehavior could lead to a last-minute burst of the behavior, a temporary escalation, but if a teacher continued, the misbehavior usually disappeared. At least, Ms. Bates and Ms. Cox weren't giving chronic disrupters the negative attention they thrived on.

There were eleven English students in the room. A new boy was dressed all in black. He wore black jeans, a heavy metal t-shirt, and thick silver links around his neck. His hair was raised in multiple spikes with hair gel. Despite his punk attire, he was a cherubic-looking kid with pink cheeks, round glasses, and a button nose.

Half of the students did free reading. They read from novels they had chosen from Ms. Bates's bookshelves. The other half completed their poetry projects at the computers. Ms. Bates set a kitchen timer for twenty minutes, and when it sounded, the groups switched. Ironically, skinny Sugar read from a young adult novel titled *Fat Kid Rules the World.* Another girl read an Oprah book selection, and a boy read a comic book.

Ms. Bates handed me the directions for the poetry project then pointed out some examples from last year that were posted on the walls. Kids chose a set of song lyrics then analyzed them from a literary perspective. They searched for examples of key terms such as irony, metaphor, and imagery. "That's the part they don't like," Ms. Bates said. The students did, however, like gluing their lyrics to posters and decorating them.

The lyrics had to be appropriate, with no violence or sexuality. Ms. Bates couldn't always understand the lyrics, though, so her backup screener was Mr. Owens. He liked the assignment so much that he once did a poetry project, himself, and analyzed a song by the Dead Kennedys.

The cherubic punk analyzed song lyrics by Metallica but Ms. Bates returned his paper. "It's not your own words. Put it in your own words," she said, which was one way of saying, "Don't plagiarize." The boy had basically cut and pasted someone's online review into his report.

Another boy worked on analyzing lyrics by AC/DC. Ms. Bates had set up a special table for him in the middle of the room. He wore a plaid flannel shirt over a t-shirt, and the flannel shoulders had fallen off. The flannel shirt drooped down his back, the whole period, and he never bothered to pull it up, although it looked cumbersome. It was a sign of apathy.

"What's the point of view?" Ms. Bates asked him, gently, but he didn't know. "It's the first person," she said.

The teacher had a conversation with another boy about returning to his regular school but he didn't want to go. "I don't want to go to Franklin," the boy said. "I live in Great Oaks, anyway."

Ms. Bates was surprised. "Really? You live in Great Oaks? Then what are you doing here?" she asked because Great Oaks wasn't even in Peachtree County.

The boy answered quickly. "My father lives in Franklin, right now, but I'm living in Great Oaks with my grandfather. He's the one who drives me to school." Ms. Bates just nodded. He was not the only student whose status as a county resident was questionable. There were at least two others on campus who resided outside of Peachtree County but still attended Peachtree Alternative School. Teachers didn't report them, though, because they thought the students were better off at the alternative school.

Next, Ms. Bates played the second half of the film, *The Outsiders.* The film starred Matt Dillon, Patrick Swayze, and Diane Lane and must have been old because the actors looked so young. Half of the class actually paid attention to the film which, at Peachtree Alternative School, qualified as a roaring success. Even though the film was set in the 1950s, it featured troubled teens. The film was based on a young adult novel of the same title, and I silently congratulated the author.

The Peachtree students paid particular attention to a gang fight, called "a rumble," in the film. The only thing that spoiled the scene was the triumphant music, afterwards. Students were also gripped by a knife scene where a hospitalized Matt Dillon viscously stabbed his pillow. In another scene, Dillon lost even more control and fired an empty pistol at a man's head, and I was disturbed to hear one of the alternative boys laughing.

Dillon's character ended up inside a convenience store, with a gun. "He's going to tear it up!" said an engrossed student. Instead, Dillon ran outside and was shot by a police officer.

Ms. Bates snapped off the television. "Okay, darlings, it's time for second period," she said.

In second period history class, Mr. Owens was covering the progressive era. The day before, they'd discussed child labor and viewed a film that included some historical photographs by Lewis Hine of kids at work. The film included testimony from a spinner in a sewing factory, who caught her hair in some machinery and was partially scalped. Mr. Owens recapped the tragedy, and students winced.

The film was so effective that Mr. Owens showed it, again, for those who'd been absent. "It's not a bad film considering it's made by a textbook company," he told me, and I gathered that he was not a big fan of history textbooks.

"I don't use textbooks very often," he told me. "There's just too much information, there." He pointed to a page in a heavy tome that was filled with fine print. "I just use them as an outline and add my own information."

James Loewen, author of *Lies My Teacher Told Me,* would agree. According to Loewen, too many high school students disliked the subject of history because of poor textbooks. Loewen's concerns about history textbooks were based on his extensive survey of the books. He thought they were too long and too adoring of American forefathers. They excluded women and minority groups and were filled with grandiose language and useless bits of information. Furthermore, they contained many mistakes because they relied, too much, on secondary and tertiary resources (journal articles and books), as opposed to historical documents. History teachers rarely made it to the end of high school history textbooks because they swept such broad expanses of time.

While the students did an assignment, Mr. Owens told me, "Next week, I'm going to cover the Spanish–American War. It's a good topic. I can make it relevant by comparing it to the war in Iraq. Terrorism sparked the war in Iraq and the explosion of the *U.S.S. Maine* sparked the Spanish–American War, although now they think it may have been an accident."

Three kids slept during Mr. Owens's lecture but three out of eleven wasn't bad. Skinny Sugar ate a bag of potato chips under a "No food or drink" sign.

Danita, the mother of twins, came in late and Mr. Owens teased her. "Are you a new student? What's your name?" He looked at the note she handed him. "Danita," he read. "Well, welcome, young lady." Danita grinned and took a seat.

Mr. Owens talked to the students about strikes, the mafia, and muckrakers, all subjects that held their attention. His voice wasn't too loud and his pace was just right. Through the wall, I heard sounds of chaos in the math teacher's room, shouts and peels of laughter, but it hardly broke our learning spell.

A girl who used to spend entire periods doing calligraphy had made a change. She now paid attention, took notes, and asked questions. Mr. Owens told us about Upton Sinclair's *The Jungle,* an exposé of meatpacking that was published in 1906. "It told how rats were ground up in the meat and people were exposed to some really, really nasty stuff." The tainted meat story led students to share their own stories of bleached chicken and altered expiration dates.

"Lawmakers read *The Jungle,*" Mr. Owens continued, "and said, 'Oh gross! We need to do something. That's nasty!' So they started inspections."

He took a moment to explain sanitary inspections of today's school cafeterias and promoted the high scores at Peachtree Alternative, thanks largely to Betty. "If inspectors these days didn't check, cooks would be flicking ashes and saying, 'Who cares about food? I'll just make slop.'" He pretended to be smoking while stirring a pot with a bored expression, and I laughed at the outrageous image, along with students.

A discussion of prohibition and bootlegging was inherently appealing to the alternative students, and Mr. Owens fed the flames by talking about the moonshine he used to drink. "My grandmother would get it from the sheriff, in a mason jar, for medical purposes. He'd confiscate it then sell it back to people to cure their warts and things. He'd put a little peppermint in it to make it taste better. My grandmother used to give it to us for just about everything: coughs, colds, whatever."

This led kids to discuss castor oil and ipecac. The girl calligrapher once had to swallow barium before an x-ray. She was winding down from her bout of studiousness. "How much more do we have to write?" she asked Mr. Owens about notetaking.

"Not much, really." He told students to write a few summarizing sentences about the Progressive Era, and most of them did.

As the kids filed out for lunch, I thought some more about textbooks. Not only were they boring but they were too expensive and students didn't always read them. "I taught college for eight years," I told Mr. Owens, "and never once used a textbook. I used articles, instead."

Mr. Owens told me that, once, he tried to stick more closely to the textbook but students didn't like it. "They complained and said they liked it better when I told stories."

"You're a born storyteller," I told him. It was part of his success as a teacher. He was a hardworking, interesting man who could pantomime and tell great stories. His elbow grease showed, as on the day he packed a trunk full of artifacts. Even disruptive students appreciated his hard work, and most of them acted accordingly. Role modeling significant effort was a key to successful classroom management. It was something, I feared, that Mr. Martin in special education was lacking, as was Mr. Wilson, the math teacher, next door.

Mr. Owen's emphasis on the cleanliness of the cafeteria gave me added confidence, and I ate my entire plate of lasagna, bread, and corn with gusto. Betty, the cafeteria manager, walked all the way to the back of the lunchroom to hand a student some extra change. "You didn't have to come back here," the kid said, with surprising sensitivity for a teenager.

"I don't mind," she told him.

During lunch, Ms. Bates complained about having to teach Kublai Khan to second period English class. "In Xanadu did Kublai Khan a stately pleasure dome decree," quoted Mr. Owens. I noticed that despite his attention to the cafeteria's sanitation score, he never ate cafeteria food, himself. He always brought homecooked Southern meals, and today he ate shrimp and cornbread.

"I can just imagine Mike's questions about the pleasure dome," Ms. Bates said about the kid who bragged about his .38 Special. She hurried to monitor the snack room, since Ms. Henderson was absent. Mr. Owens went to make copies, which left me at the table with Mr. Wilson, the math teacher. The two of us ate in silence. He looked especially weary, that morning, and I was sure that the commotion in his room had something to do with it. He finished his food and pushed back his chair to keep a better eye on the kids.

He was unsuccessful at keeping cans of soda from flying across the lunchroom, and I was uncomfortable sitting across from an ineffective teacher, with my back to the kids. My protectors, Ms. Bates and Mr. Owens, were missing.

NOVEMBER 20

I picked up illustrator Ashley Bryan from his sister's home. He wore a beige suit and a bolo tie over an African print shirt. People had been teasing him, lately, about his unruly hair. "I need a haircut," he told me. "They say I look like a black Albert Einstein."

Ashley was eighty years old but looked much younger and was amazingly spry. He was born in the Bronx to parents who emigrated from Antigua. Ashley grew up in a loving household that supported his artistic talents. His mother kept a beautiful, flower-filled home, and his father had a quirky sense of humor. As a child, he would make picture books and give them to relatives as presents.

After high school, Ashley applied to a prestigious art school but was rejected because he was black, even though he had the top-ranked art portfolio. Still, he kept on sketching and painting. During World War II, he kept art supplies in his gas mask and would sketch fellow soldiers during moments of rest.

I had known Ashley since I was a teenager. Ashley and my mother had traveled to Kenya and South Africa together to promote the development of children's libraries.

After World War II, Ashley lived in New York City and helped raise his sister's seven children. He taught art at the Wiltwyck School for boys in New Jersey, an early alternative school for emotionally disturbed students and students on parole, before moving on to teach art at Dartmouth College.

Ashley recalled his alternative school days, "I knew if I could teach art to those boys, I could teach anyone," he said then gave me some valuable advice. "They try to get a rise out of you. They're so used to adults responding in anger. If you keep responding to them gently, over time, they'll begin to soften."

Ashley recommended that I read *The Freedom Writer's Diary* by Erin Gruwell, a young woman who taught at-risk youth. She struggled to teach the kids, at first, but the turning point came when she began teaching them about the Holocaust. It unleashed a flood of compassion and motivated students to begin writing. They even wrote letters to Zlata Filipovic, a survivor of the war in Bosnia and, ultimately, raised enough funds to have her visit their school.

When Ashley heard about the loss of the school librarian, he said, wearily, "Isn't that always the way it is?"

We pulled up outside the school, and Ashley grabbed his leather satchel, filled with surprises. I carried in free copies of his books for teachers and a bird mobile from his publisher's office. The mobile promoted his book, *Beautiful Blackbird.* I held it aloft, and colorful cardboard birds dangled beside me.

High school students stared at us, in the hall, and the principal greeted us warmly. She had done her homework by watching a National Geographic video about Ashley. "I know all about you," she said, pumping his hand. "You were born in the Bronx, and you live on an island in Maine. We're honored to have you." She put her arm around me and added, "And we appreciate Mary's being here."

Ms. Henderson escorted us down the hall to a conference room, where I hung up the mobile. We also displayed thirty of Ashley's children's books, arranged chairs, and waited for the students to arrive.

At first, Ms. Henderson had been hesitant to let the special education students hear the artist, fearing they'd be too disrespectful, but Ms. Hackett had talked her into it. I gave Ms. Hackett a lot of credit for her persistence and preparation. She had shown the special education students a documentary about Ashley Bryan, early that morning.

Ms. Henderson tried to warn him about the special education students. "These are kids with severe discipline problems," she told him. "If they're too disruptive, just let me know."

"I'll just keep going," Ashley told her.

The first student to filter in was little Leon, who surprised me by beaming at Ashley, shaking his hand, and sitting in the very front row. Jarrod and a boy I didn't know also sat in front. The rest of the teens, though, sat in the very back until Ms. Henderson ordered them to move up. "How old are you?" a boy shouted rudely but Ashley either ignored him or didn't hear him.

During his presentation, Ashley emphasized aspects of his artwork and his life as a black man. He described how he cut blocks for black-and-white block prints that he used in his first two books of African American spirituals. Even the musical notes were block prints.

He dipped into his leather satchel, withdrew a recorder, and played a few spirituals. When he finished playing "Angels Watching Over Me," a boy in back said, "Amen," and the mostly sullen crowd began to melt.

The teenagers snapped their fingers as Ashley performed a rap song. Next, he proudly recited "My People" by Langston Hughes and told students how important it was for them to celebrate their cultural heritage.

As he recited "Madam and the Rent Man," also by Langston Hughes, students were literally on the edges of their seats. I suspected it was a poem that too many of them could relate to. Many of them lived in poverty, and the rent man trying to collect debt was probably all too familiar. Students laughed at the line, " I said, 'Listen, before I'd pay, I'd go to Hades and rot away.'"

Ashley then read his picture book *Beautiful Blackbird* to the teenagers. He held the book aloft, open to a spread where an array of bright birds surrounded and admired a lone blackbird. The other birds praised blackbird's glossy feathers.

In the story, based on a Zambian folktale, blackbird gave some of his black color to the other birds. He painted black dots and black stripes, all the while telling them that their insides, not their outsides, mattered most. "Black is beautiful, uh-huh, uh-huh," Ashley read. "Black is beautiful." The message to his readers, to love themselves, could not have been clearer.

By the time he finished his presentation, the group sat in awed silence. Ms. Hackett and the other special education teachers were grinning, and even a former gang member was sitting with his mouth open.

"How old are you?" a boy asked, again, and, that time, his question wasn't meant to be rude.

"Age doesn't matter," Ashley told him. "You can be fifteen and seem very old because you don't care about anything or you can have a passion for something and seem young." He paused to let the message sink in then told the students, "I am eighty years old."

Ms. Pearl, who had an Ashley Bryan picture taped to the front of her desk, let out a gasp. She couldn't help herself. "My goodness," she said. "I thought you were much younger."

Teachers received autographed books, and we arranged to take a photo of the students with the illustrator in the middle. Ironically, the most disruptive teens, the ones who had begun the session by making snorting noises, jostled to be by Ashley's side. I stood on the fringes of a group shot with a beaming Jarrod's arm around me.

As students left the room, Mr. Martin tapped the table beside me in a wordless acknowledgment of a good show. We stopped by the cafeteria so Ashley could meet the lunchroom and custodial staff. He autographed our remaining books for their children and grandchildren.

In the car on the way home, Ashley showed me a poem that Jarrod had written and slipped into his pocket. Ashley wrote a quick note back to Jarrod, for me to deliver. "Keep on writing," Ashley told him.

Lovely songs and poetry echoed in my head, all evening.

NOVEMBER 22

My husband and I ran into the academic counselor and her husband at a barbecue restaurant, and I shook the man's hand, vigorously. "Your wife is wonderful!" I told him. Ms. Wilkins filled so many important roles at the school: advisor, advocate, community liaison, even assistant principal.

"You missed a lot of action, yesterday," she told me. "They brought in drug-sniffing dogs." She found it particularly interesting that the officers spoke Dutch to the dogs so students wouldn't understand the instructions.

"The dogs can't sniff students," she told me. "But they can sniff around the building. You should have seen the kids. One of them had marijuana in his sock. He passed it to another student who tried to hide it in a tailpipe. A teacher saw the whole thing!" The counselor could not hide her satisfaction.

NOVEMBER 29

The principal and her staff had been invited to give a presentation about the school at a Save Our Students meeting. I slipped into a back row of the conference room, as Ms. Wilkins began. "I am the longest surviving member of this staff," she said, and the audience laughed. She told us about the history and demographics of the school. Peachtree Alternative School began almost ten years ago and one of the flaws, back then, according to Ms. Wilkins, was "a boring worksheet curriculum."

She told the audience the reasons some of the students were at the school. The offenses were many, and she read quickly from a long list. "Thirty-three are here for chronic disruption. Eleven are here for drug possession, sale, or use. Nine are special education severe disrupters, eight are behind academically two or more years, five are here for sex crimes, five possessed a knife on campus, and three assaulted school employees."

She paused to catch her breath. "There's more. We also have three assaults, two burglaries, two terroristic threats, and one attempted rape." The counselor couldn't stay to answer questions and hustled out the door. To hear offenses spelled out in a rapid-fire manner was startling, and the room was quiet for a moment.

A few alternative students had been recruited to say some good things about the school but they mumbled badly and were hard to hear. I caught that they liked the comparatively smaller classes and individual attention from teachers. The most interesting student speaker was Brandy's buddy Heather. Apparently, Heather was at Peachtree Alternative for making terroristic threats at her old school. She confessed to Save Our Students that she had "an anger problem" and was working on controlling her temper.

Heather was followed by her mother who said, "My daughter made a mistake. I cried my eyes out when I heard she had to come here but a policeman told me to give the school a chance. Now, as far as I'm concerned, she can stay here forever.

"She doesn't talk back, any more," Heather's mother said. "She thinks she's beautiful." She gestured towards her tall blonde daughter who really was a beautiful girl. "My daughter used to think she was ugly but now she's beautiful." It was nice to know that at Peachtree Alternative School, teachers such as Ms. Cox and Ms. W-J, were helping Heather's self-esteem.

Heather's mother kept on raving. "This school is wonderful. If they close this school, all of these kids are going to be down at his station." She pointed to the police chief, who was sitting in the audience.

More adults stood, spontaneously, to echo her sentiments about the school. A long-time volunteer called Miss Stacy banged on a table. Miss Stacy taught a nutrition and etiquette class to the high school students. Sometimes, the class culminated in a free luncheon at a fancy restaurant, which was a big incentive for students to study.

Miss Stacy spoke in a thick southern drawl. "These teachers love these students." She jabbed the tabletop to emphasize her point. "They love them." She paused and looked around the room. "If this school closed, where would kids go? They'd probably go rob a store or kill someone."

A parole officer spoke, next. "This is one of the best schools I've seen. I've seen high schools that don't work and alternative schools that don't work. This school works because everyone cares. They work as a team.

"I don't think Ms. Henderson ever goes home," he joked, and the group laughed. "She really loves this place."

The former librarian, who had lost his job over the summer, stood and spoke in the voice of a preacher. "This is a good school. The staff is dedicated to the task. It would be a sin if the school closed because I know it's an asset to the community. Put in a good word for the school," he told the audience.

The principal, who had been in and out of the room, several times, explained her absences. "I'm going to be frank with you," she said. "You've come on a bad morning. We've just had a fight in the cafeteria. A teacher was hurt, and the students went to DJJ," she said, meaning the Department of Juvenile Justice. I looked over at the police chief, a burly man with a shaved head, but he didn't move a muscle. "We think the fight stemmed from a football game, this weekend.

"We have a tough job," Ms. Henderson said. "And you wonder why we're not stressed . . . why we *are* stressed," she corrected herself. "I don't think the public knows what we deal with on a daily basis."

The principal concluded the presentation by combating labeling. "Someone once said that we deal with hoodlums, here. We don't have hoodlums. We have kids who have problems, kids at risk. We believe in what we're doing."

NOVEMBER 30

"Who are you observing, this morning?" Ms. Bates asked me.

"Ms. Henderson."

"That's good. I don't even think the teachers know exactly what she does."

The principal and I sat at a table during breakfast, and she called over a girl who had been using foul language on the bus. The girl had been swearing at her cousin, who was also in the school. "I heard you called him a motherfucker," said Ms. Henderson. "Is that how you speak to your cousin?" The girl nodded and Ms. Henderson frowned.

"We don't talk like that, here," the principal said. "I'm giving you a warning and if I have to give you another warning then I'm filing a juvenile complaint. Do you hear me?"

"I won't do it, again. I promise," said the girl, surprisingly contrite for an alternative student.

I followed the principal into a small conference room across from the front office. A middle school girl was sitting with her father, as well as the art teacher and a deputy from the sheriff's department. The girl had called a special education student "a fucking retard" then shoved Ms. Cox.

Ms. Henderson dealt with the first issue. "A teacher heard you say it," she told the girl. "I know he said something to you first but you didn't have to talk back. You have to learn to control your anger.

"And calling him a retard can be hurtful. Can you imagine how it would feel if you were in special education and someone said that to you?" The girl bit her lip. She had a much older father, and he sat quietly, looking ashamed.

Ms. Henderson glanced at her paperwork. "This is not the first time I've had to talk to you. I have stacks and stacks of paperwork on you, and I'm getting tired of it. And we have another issue to deal with—what you did to Ms. Cox.

The art teacher was hurt and angry. "She shoved me," she said. "She was just being ugly."

I knew the girl liked Ms. Cox because I'd seen her volunteering in the art room, after school. Maybe that was why the art teacher found the girl's behavior so painful.

Ms. Henderson and the officer played good cop/bad cop. "Okay," Ms. Henderson said. "We have two issues on the table. Tell me what it looks like from your perspective, Corporal Smith."

The man leaned forward. "We can definitely charge her with profanity. That's against a city ordinance. I'm still deciding on the battery case. I'm not sure about that one, yet. I'll have to look into it."

Ms. Henderson swiveled back towards the girl. "I've decided to just make a note of the incident with Ms. Cox." She scribbled on her notepad. "I'm also going to suspend you for nine days." Nine days was the longest suspension I'd heard of at Peachtree Alternative School. Three or five days was more typical. The principal wrote down the sentence then passed it over for the father to sign. "Do you have anything to add?" she asked him.

"I gave her a whoopin' at home," was all he said. No one said anything about the corporal punishment, and I hoped it wasn't brutal.

Another parent meeting was with a high school boy and his father. Both males wore dirty, tattered clothing. The boy was the withdrawn student from Ms. Bates's English class, who wore the same droopy plaid shirt. His father was unshaven and had a grimy baseball cap. Ms. Henderson dropped the three of us off in the media center, where we waited for Ms. Bates.

The English teacher came in and reviewed the boy's academic standing. "Rick has slept through most of his classes," she told his father. "That's why he's done so poorly. He also walks out the door and wanders down in the hall when he's not supposed to." I gathered that Rick had already been suspended and we were just having a "check in" meeting. "Here's what you'll have to do to pass my class," Ms. Bates said. She told Rick his assignments in a gentle voice.

Ms. Wilkins replaced Ms. Bates at the meeting. "I'm going to write a corrective action plan," she said. "Here's what we've already done," she pointed to some handwriting on her form, "and here's what we're going to do."

"I see you've already had detention, phone conferences, suspension, and now we've had a sit-down parent conference," she told Rick. "There's not much more we can do. We don't have a lot of consequences, around here. We don't have in-school suspension, any more, since we don't have enough staff. All we have left is expulsion. That would mean you'd be out of Peachtree County Schools for a year then you'd really be behind." She wrote expulsion in capital letters.

"I'm going to suggest you go to group counseling. We have it here, in the media center, on Fridays," she told Rick. "There are a lot of other boys so you won't be the only one."

She turned to Rick's father. "How does that sound?"

Rick's father agreed to group counseling for his son, and Ms. Wilkins spotted the man's tattoos. "What does that spell on your knuckles?" she asked, leaning forward. The man showed her his left hand that spelled H - A- T- E but hid his other hand under his jacket. "Were you in prison?" the counselor asked.

"More than once," the man said.

"Did you get that in prison?" Ms. Wilkins asked about the letters.

"Nah, I got that when I divorced my wife. It was for her," he said and chuckled.

Ms. Wilkins apologized. "I didn't mean to embarrass you," she said. "I just wonder about these things. What do you do, now?"

Rick's father was an independent contractor who did odd jobs, and Ms. Wilkins said she might hire him to help around the house. "I sometimes hire students' relatives," she said. "I hired Chris Moser's father to paint my house," she told Rick.

I realized that the woman was serious. She would take a gamble and hire a former felon. I admired her for being so polite to a parent. And it was a smart move to get to know parents better. The more connected teachers and parents were, the more likely it was that students would graduate. The counselor had a big heart but, sometimes, big-hearted people got hurt.

In the neighborhood where I grew up, a woman was stabbed to death by her newly hired gardener, a former homeless man. Elizabeth Smart was kidnapped by a handyman with a similar background. You had to carefully balance your compassion and personal safety.

"What are our three rules?" the counselor asked Rick, who didn't remember.

"The three Bs," she said. "Be here. Be passing. Behave," she recited.

I sat awkwardly throughout the whole corrective action process. I didn't realize what I was getting into when I first sat down and, the longer I sat, the harder it was for me to leave, inconspicuously. I decided to see the process through to the very end.

Mr. Owens replaced the counselor and shook hands with Rick's father. On the father's right hand, I saw a swastika tattoo. He had tried to change it into a square with four cells, by adding some lines, but the swastika was still prominent. "If you have a problem with other teachers, go talk to them," Mr. Owens told Rick. "Don't take it out on me." He then reviewed the work that Rick needed to do in order to catch up.

Rick and his father left, and I stopped by the counselor's office. She showed me how thick Rick's file was but didn't open it. Rick had problem behaviors dating back to the first grade. I told the counselor about the swastika, and she said, "Now you see the kind of parents we're dealing with. At least, he was embarrassed about it."

I rejoined the principal who was making her regular rounds. She had to see and be seen. We went next door to a preschool building that I'd never visited before. There were no windows in the Pre-K classrooms, not a single one, and I had trouble spotting the exits because the walls were plastered with student artwork. The preschool was actually one giant room partitioned into eight smaller rooms. It made me feel claustrophobic, and I wondered how it wasn't a fire hazard. Surely, it had been inspected. No wonder the school superintendent once referred to the county preschool building as "a maze."

I watched a couple of alternative high school girls assist preschoolers with an art project. Helping in preschool was a service learning project for some of the better behaved alternative students.

As Ms. Henderson and I left the preschool building, she told me about a conversation she'd just had with Corporal Smith. She had heard that a student had a mint container filled with marijuana, and she wanted to do a search.

"We've done it before and ended up with all kinds of things like knives and brass knuckles."

He recommended that she hold off, though, for legal reasons. The student was one of the few, in the school, who had a wealthy father who tended to hire expensive lawyers.

"I'm having to pick my battles, today, and this is not one of them," Ms. Henderson said, and I was kind of sorry to miss a shakedown. "I'm going to question students, though."

We walked down 200 Hall, and Ms. Henderson poked her head in a few doors. "Don't sit on the desk," she told Mr. Martin. "You're a teacher so act like one."

We headed down the hall past long rows of empty metal lockers with combinations long forgotten. Ms. Henderson poked her head in another classroom and greeted the teacher, while Mr. Martin passed us, dragging Derrick, the arsonist. The boy kicked lockers the entire way.

At the intersection of 200 Hall and the Derelict Hall was a corner room, otherwise known as Time Out. I hadn't seen it, before. The walls of the room were painted dark gray. The paraprofessional, who was so generous with her hugs, was in there with a handful of special education students, and she was looking frazzled. A pounding came from somewhere else.

I looked around to find the source, and the principal opened a connecting door that led into another room containing a solitary confinement cell. The cell was dark inside and had a small, square window. Derrick was inside, pounding over and over again on the door. The cell was double bolted on the outside.

I felt physically ill, as if someone had punched me in the stomach. Here I was thinking Peachtree Alternative was so therapeutic, and it had a terrible secret. Solitary confinement was an ultimate punishment. *What if children were afraid of the dark? What if they were claustrophobic?* "Most people have no idea this is here," Ms. Henderson said. I certainly hadn't, and I had been inside the building for three months.

Derrick was a boy who had listened to me read aloud. He had even colored a picture for me. *Why was he locked up? Didn't all that pounding scare the other children?* It was the kind of set up you saw in a mental institution, not a school! I was in shock. I backed into the hall, and the principal followed.

We walked down the Derelict Hall, which was dark and icy cold. Ms. Henderson called a custodian, on her radio, to board up some broken windows that were letting in cold air. Ms. Wilkins met us, around the corner on 100 Hall, to report that a boy had slapped a girl. "She doesn't want to make a big deal out of it," the counselor said, "but she still has a handprint on her cheek."

"That's not up to her to decide," the principal said. "That behavior is uncalled for."

I spotted Derrick, later on, in the cafeteria and was relieved he had been released. He saw me and came over with his arms open for a hug. "Hey, fellow," I said, hugging him and patting his back. It was a bittersweet moment. Here was a boy who wanted hugs yet, repeatedly, threatened to hurt people. *What would happen to the poor kid?*

Ms. Henderson did paperwork during lunch and worried about the large number of students pouring into the school. "We have four new students in special education," she told me, "and Mr. Martin's class is already full. Ms. Cox's class is full, too. She has as many students as she can handle." The principal rubbed her forehead. "I don't know where all these kids are coming from." She told me that an elementary school even tried to send over a disruptive fifth grader but she refused to have him.

I waited by the front desk while Ms. Henderson made phone calls in her office. A middle schooler plunked down beside me. He was being sent home for ringworm, and his parole officer was picking him up.

Our next meeting was held in a large conference room off 200 Hall, one usually reserved for tribunals. Ms. Henderson and I joined Ms. Wilkins and a boy named Alan. Both women had notepads, and Ms. Henderson began by asking questions. She knew how to interrogate. A police officer had given her a book on interrogation tactics, and she studied body language. She looked for eyes shifting away, and she waited for students to fill in long pauses. "Why are you here, Alan?" she asked.

"Possession of marijuana."

"And have you smoked marijuana since you've been here?"

"No. I don't want to mess up, again."

"Have you bought or sold marijuana?"

"No."

"Tell her about the salt," Ms. Wilkins told Alan.

"I snorted some salt," Alan said. "People dared me to so I did it, and it hurt."

"You did it twice, didn't you?" said the counselor, and he nodded.

"So you gave in to peer pressure," said the principal. "That concerns me, Alan, because at some point you're going to need to stand up for yourself and be your own person." She rested her elbows on the table and tapped her fingertips together.

Both women were speaking slowly. They leaned back in their cushioned chairs, a perk of the tribunal room, and the counselor put her hands behind her head. Alan looked equally calm, to me, concerned and earnest.

"Let me give you a hypothetical situation," began Ms. Henderson. "Suppose someone in this school offered you a marijuana cigarette, what would you do?"

"I'd probably smoke it but only once."

"Only *once?*" said Ms. Henderson, raising her voice. "Let me tell you what concerns me about 'only once.' I've heard crack addicts say 'only once.' I've heard alcoholics at the shelter where I volunteer say 'only once.' They'll have only one beer then three then twelve. 'Only once' is a dangerous thing to say."

She thought some more. "Let me tell you, Alan, that Ms. Wilkins and I know everything that goes on in this building. *Everything.* And we heard you have pot. Is it true?"

"No," said Alan. "I wouldn't do that."

"Then why would someone say that?"

"Maybe to get me in trouble. I heard a student got thrown against the wall, last year, during a drug bust. Maybe someone wants that to happen to me."

"I've been here four years," said the principal, "and Ms. Wilkins has been here ten, and I can tell you that never happened. That's not how we operate.

"You're suggesting someone is spreading rumors," Ms. Henderson said, and Alan nodded. She turned to Ms. Wilkins. "Do you have anything to say?" she asked her colleague.

The conversation took a major turn when the counselor removed her glasses and fixed Alan with a stare. "Tell me where the good places are to hide drugs," she said. That was when I realized that the women didn't believe him.

The room was freezing, and I'd never seen the women be so intimidating. It was a cold day and the heat wasn't working. The weather, combined with the tenseness of the situation, started me shivering. I pressed my knees together under the table and looked at my fingernails, which were beginning to turn blue. I was trembling, and I wasn't even guilty.

"I don't know," said Alan. I sat beside him and watched his Adam's apple bob. Under the table, he gripped the base of his shirt in his hands.

"Are you sure you can't think of anyplace?" asked Ms. Wilkins. Alan finally suggested that inside the computers might be a good place.

Ms. Henderson and the counselor gave each other a long look. Finally, the principal said, "I'm going to let you go now, Alan, but I want to emphasize that you're one of the lucky ones, around here. You have two parents and come from a good home. That's more than a lot of our students. We have kids in foster care and kids who are homeless. You should appreciate what you've got because you have more opportunities than most students. You're a smart young man so act like one."

Ms. Wilkins escorted Alan out. "What did you think?" the principal asked me.

"He looked pretty innocent."

"I think he's lying," she said. "He's lied to us before."

The counselor returned with another boy in tow. He sat and looked at his knees, and I looked at them, too. Despite the cold, he was wearing blue jean shorts, and his knees were knobby. I tried not to be a distraction, sitting across from the two women and beside the student, but I was trembling. I hoped it was imperceptible.

"Have you been smoking pot around here?" Ms. Henderson asked, and the boy shook his head.

"Have you seen anyone with pot?" The boy paused before saying he hadn't. "That was a long pause," Ms. Henderson said. "Are you sure?" We all waited for him to confess.

"Well, maybe one person," he said.

"What was it in?" Ms. Wilkins asked.

"A mint container," the boy said. Now, they were getting somewhere. The boy described the container.

"Was the person black or white?" asked the counselor.

"He was white."

"We know it was in Mr. Wilson's room," said the principal. She gave the boy her speech about knowing everything that went on in the school. "Where was Mr. Wilson and why weren't you studying?" she asked, and the boy told her the teacher was just sitting in front.

"We didn't have anything to do." That didn't surprise me because I had visited the math teacher's sterile classroom and knew he just gave worksheets. I regularly heard chaos coming from his room.

"Why don't you tell us who had the pot," the principal said. The boy didn't say anything so Ms. Henderson resorted to issuing a legitimate threat. She asked how old the boy was. He was sixteen. "Right now, you're a juvenile," Ms. Henderson said, "but let me tell you what happens when you turn seventeen. If you commit a crime at seventeen then you go to prison in handcuffs, not juvenile detention but prison. That is not a place where you want to be."

The boy said that Alan had the pot. "You did the right thing by cooperating," Ms. Henderson told him. "Now, we're going to bring in another student so you're not singled out for telling. If they ask what went on in here, just tell them you can't talk about it."

"And another thing," Ms. Wilkins added. She leaned far across the table to make her point. She warned the boy about a preadolescent girl who had a crush on him. "She's only twelve years old," the counselor said, "and the best thing you can do is stay away from her. Do you hear me? Stay far away. If she crooks her little finger and tries to get you to go outside, *don't go.*"

"I know," the boy said. He had tried to stay away from the precocious girl but it was hard because she rode the bus with him and her assigned seat was directly across from his. "I try to just look out the window. She keeps calling my house, though."

"That is harassment, and we can talk to the police," said Ms. Wilkins.

The women interrogated one more boy, just for show. He was eighteen and didn't know anything. After he left, we looked at one another.

"Alan is a good liar, isn't he?" Ms. Henderson asked. "I'm going to give this information to his parole officer and let her do a drug test." She complained to Ms. Wilkins. "This is all because that Mr. Wilson does *nothing* in his room. He doesn't keep an eye on them, much less keep them busy!"

The school day ended, and I lingered to avoid the rush of kids. I was disturbed by having my romantic notions of therapeutic alternative schooling dashed in one afternoon. Even the computer teacher, a former counselor, noticed that something was wrong with me. He saw me walking down the hall with my arms crossed, still shivering.

He pulled me aside, and I steeled myself for an assessment. "I notice body language," he said, "and I notice you've been rather closed off, lately." I didn't welcome his assessment and would rather have been left alone.

"I've been subbing in special education," I told him.

"That explains a lot," he said and looked so sympathetic that I couldn't help but blurt out more.

"We had a kid, in there, who banged his head against the wall," I told him, "and I just saw that solitary confinement cell. It's frightening."

The computer teacher agreed. "I know. I don't go down there."

"And, right now, I'm cold. I'm just cold," I added.

"Well, I have a warm jacket you can always borrow." He patted my arm. "Thank you for sharing."

I went home, petted my dog, and made some hot tea.

Chapter 5

December

DECEMBER 9

"We're up to sixteen students," Ms. W-J told me about her science class, and I cringed in sympathy. "It's been rough," she added. She was a nine-year veteran who rarely complained so I knew things were bad.

Ms. W-J warned students to be quiet as we headed to her room. We passed a closed door with a sign that read, "Do Not Disturb. Proceeding In Progress."

"We have tribunals almost every day, now," Ms. W-J told me. They were a serious disciplinary measure at Peachtree Alternative School—a last step, after a number of disciplinary problems had been documented. During tribunals, a variety of adults determined whether or not a student would be expelled.

A colorful contraption was set up in front of the room. It was a big box with four colored lights. Four cords snaked from the box to desks, ending in buzzers. We were going to play Science Jeopardy, and today's topic was metals. There was an odd number of students, so I paired up with Brandy. She and I were the blue team.

We were allowed to use the textbook to look up answers. Ms. W-J sat in front, and we began. Everyone was grinning. The categories are "identification," "formation," and "resources." I couldn't answer any of the initial questions, which worried me because I was a certified science teacher. The kids put me to shame and had a grand time buzzing away and shouting out answers such as "What is lava?" and "What is fluorescence?"

My partner Brandy did a good job in the mining category, and the room rang with laughter. A student came in late, and I offered him my seat beside Brandy but he didn't want it. Instead, he slid his head and arms inside a gray sweatshirt, like a turtle.

Figure 5.   Isolation Cubbies in Special Education.

Ms. W-J asked a final bonus question. "Talc is used in what household product?" The kids were stumped and flipped through their textbooks, in vain.

I finally signaled Brandy to press our buzzer, and a blue light glowed on Ms. W-J's box. "What is baby powder?" I said. We tallied our scores and with a whopping 6000 bonus points for the baby powder answer, Brandy and I were declared the winners. None of the kids complained that it was unfair having an adult win.

"Tomorrow, we'll do it without textbooks," said Ms. W-J, who was filled with good ideas. Students had even made volcanoes, in her class, which a lot of science teachers shied away from because they were so messy. The ceiling and walls had been decorated like a rainforest, since I last visited. Fluffy white clouds dangled from the ceiling and colorful pictures of poison dart frogs covered the walls.

There had been a gang fight in the neighborhood, earlier that day. As a precautionary measure, we had four uniformed officers outside the lunch-room rather than the usual one. The men on the S.W.A.T. team wore bullet-proof vests.

The peanut butter and jelly in our sandwiches was mixed together to reduce sogginess. I stood to get a plastic knife before I remembered that we only had forks and spoons.

The latecomer to science class was still in turtle mode. He sat alone, hunched over a table, not eating. I asked Ms. W-J about him, and she told me that he had tried to go AWOL, that morning. With all the officers around, though, he was quickly retrieved.

"He's a stoner," said a boy, who had been eavesdropping, before shooting past with his tray.

Ms. Cox, the art teacher who was eating lunch with us, looked at the boy curled inside his sweatshirt, widened her eyes, and told me. "You can't save every student. I didn't know that, at first."

Back in Ms. W-J's room, students had free time. We listened to Christmas carols on the radio, and a boy hummed along. It was a peaceful afternoon. Some boys played checkers, and Brandy wrote in her journal. She had a terrible hacking cough and didn't bother to cover her mouth.

"Are you coming to my house, this afternoon?" one boy asked another.

"I have to stay out of trouble. Every time we get together, you get me in trouble," his friend said, which was a remarkably mature response.

A clump of boys in a corner began a loud, rapid-fire conversation that I could barely understand because of the thick dialect. Ms. W-J looked up from her desk, though. "Lose that word!" she snapped at the boys.

"What word?" a boy asked, all innocence.

"The N-word," said Ms. W-J. The boys went back to talking nonstop, with barely a breath. I caught the words "gun" and "jail" and the phrase, "he was touching my sister."

"Gentlemen, find something else to talk about," said Ms. W-J, which put a stop to the conversation.

The day ended with gym class. As middle schoolers left the building, the counselor introduced a new sixth grader to Ms. W-J. The small white girl was wearing boys' clothing. The sides of her head were shaved and she wore the rest of her hair in a ponytail. I studied the girl and wondered if the influx of kids would ever stop.

It was cold in the gymnasium. There was no heat, and temperatures, lately, had been below freezing, which was rare in the Deep South. The kids playing basketball managed to stay warm but the ones on the bleachers were shivering.

I huddled with Ms. Pearl, from special education, and longed for a cup of coffee. "We've had a hard nine weeks," Ms. Pearl told me without prompting. "especially Mr. Martin. They're hiring an extra paraprofessional because he has so many kids in there." Ms. Pearl spotted trouble, across the gym, and headed towards it. "Hey!" she shouted. "Put those dice away. There's no gambling."

I watched the new girl play basketball. She wore a football jersey and sagging blue jeans over boxers. The girl caught me watching and flashed a brilliant smile that caught me off guard. So often, the alternative students scowled. Her broad beam made me feel guilty about my own frequent surliness.

Turtle boy came out of his gray sweatshirt and began patrolling the bleachers behind me, wildly swinging a baseball bat. His behavior was unnerving. I moved away but Ms. W-J pursued him and made him give up the bat. Two maintenance men came in, climbed to the top of the bleachers, and examined a heating unit near the ceiling. They discussed lighting a pilot light but waited until a third man brought a fire extinguisher. Seeing that, I started directing kids to the front doors. In such a neglected gymnasium, an explosion wasn't entirely unlikely.

A narrow strip of glass in the front door was covered in red spray paint. I peered outside and saw that some middle schoolers were smoking.

The day ended, and kids began boarding school buses. White kids filled the Holly Springs bus, and black kids filled the one headed for Franklin.

A boy with a blonde buzz cut joined me on the front steps and tried to destroy the awning over our heads, by rocking a pole back and forth. The concrete base began to crack and the metal, above us, made terrible screeching noises. My adult presence was not the remotest deterrent, and I was momentarily shocked into silence. I jumped out of the way so as not to be crushed by collapsing metal. It was major vandalism, not to mention suicidal, but the boy quit when his ride pulled up.

DECEMBER 11

Mr. Martin and Ms. Hackett had switched to a larger cubby room. "I had to beg Ms. Henderson for this room," Ms. Hackett told me. "Friday was the worst day I ever had, and I had to do something." After seeing the solitary confinement cell, the cubbies in special education classrooms hardly bothered me.

The names of eleven boys were written on the board. Several boys were new to me. There was a desk for Ms. Hackett, a rectangular table for Mr. Martin, and student desks in every single cubby. Ms. Hackett made the boys push their desks further back inside the cubbies so they couldn't distract one another.

"My cousin got electrocuted by a space heater," Tom, the fisherman, announced as he adjusted his desk. "She got fifteen hundred volts." Space heaters were a hazard among the county's low-income residents, many of whom did not have central heating, and burns and fires were common in winter months.

"I'm sorry." said Mr. Martin. "Was she hurt?" Tom said his cousin had burns on her feet and was in an intensive care unit.

New rules were posted on a large white board beside Ms. Hackett's desk. They read, "No talking at any time! (This includes singing, rapping, beating.) No one gets out of cubbies *at all!* Each time one of the rules is broken, you will receive a check beside your name."

The boys had misbehaved to the point where they were being drastically restricted. Mr. Martin and Ms. Hackett had piles of worksheets for them to do. A row of crisp file folders lined the base of the board, and each folder had a boy's name on it. When they completed their work, they had to ask permission to put it in their folders.

A few students attempted to speak without raising their hands but quickly received check marks by their names. Check marks meant extra work. The boys began doing seatwork in silence.

Ms. Hackett turned and whispered to me about the new set up. "This may look mean but I had to do something. They were out of control." *The fact that they were severely disruptive was no surprise to me. I'd seen the chaos, myself.* The captive audience in cubbies was perfect for reading aloud a good children's book but that probably would have been more of a reward than a punishment. It was awkward watching the boys watch me. With their views of each other obstructed, they had nothing to look at except worksheets, windows, and adults in the room.

Andrew, the boy who had thrown a trashcan, had been throwing food at breakfast. "He'll calm down once his medicine kicks in," Ms. Hackett told me.

Andrew was a real handful. He was a handsome boy whose behavior made him frightening. He wore an unusual outfit for a cold morning, baggy tropical-print shorts and a checkered flannel shirt so he appeared to be a mixture of surfer dude and lumberjack. In his right ear, he sported a fake diamond stud, like so many of the boys in school.

The boy who tricked me into thinking he was urinating arrived late. He explained that he had to do his own laundry and the dryer wasn't working. He also told us, matter-of-factly, that someone had tried to poison his uncle by putting anti-freeze in the man's coffee. It was another sordid tale that rang true and was another reminder of the kids' tragic lives.

Somehow, the boys looked smaller inside their cubbies. Some finished their worksheets but others had a hard time focusing. An overweight boy leaned back in his chair and kept banging his head on the concrete wall behind him. *Thump! Thump! Thump!* He then began writing on the wall.

Ms. Hackett's desk was covered in spools of ribbon and lace. She was tying ribbons into large bows, deftly making decorations for the school Christmas tree. A new boy watched her. "Can I have some ribbon?" he asked.

"No," said Ms. Hackett. It was not her nature to stifle creativity so I knew she'd been pushed to the limit.

The boy tried, again. "Can I just come talk to you?"

"Why?" asked Ms. Hackett.

"Just to talk." The boy gave her a sweet smile but she held firm with her regime. I had no idea where Mr. Martin was during all of the disciplining and, once again, the hard work fell on his parapro.

A boy's creativity, spawned from desperate boredom, made me laugh out loud. He must have seen the latest werewolf film because he was entertaining himself by making a set of ten paper claws. He made vicious faces and wiggled the claws wickedly in the air.

Ms. Hackett confiscated a rubber band from a boy, who whined to have it back. "No, sir," said Ms. Hackett. "As soon as you did this," she demonstrated by stretching the rubber band between her thumb and forefinger and aiming, "it became a weapon."

Little Leon had zipped his head and arms inside a red parka and was playing a video game, while Tom drew a marijuana leaf on the cover of his notebook. Next, Tom began disassembling a ballpoint pen to make a blow pipe. He ripped off bits of paper and chewed them for ammunition, until Ms. Hackett noticed. "Put that pen away," she barked, and Tom tucked the blow pipe behind his ear.

Someone kicked balls of paper into the center of the room. "Pick those up and put 'em in the trash," Ms. Hackett bellowed, and a boy scooped them out of the way. "It's sad I have to watch you so closely that I can't even make Christmas decorations."

Someone made farting noises. "No bodily noises," said Ms. Hackett. She looked up from tying a bow and spotted a boy with his feet against the wall. "Put your feet down," she ordered, and I could see that the guard duty was beginning to wear her down.

The boy with paper claws repeatedly scraped his notebook and made horrible faces. Next, he made a paper hat, and I had to admire his ingenuity.

The boredom was killing most of the people in the room. In punishing the kids, adults were punishing themselves.

Lunchtime finally rolled around. The boys lined up eagerly but were sorry to learn that they wouldn't be eating in the cafeteria. They couldn't mingle with their friends and would have to bring their lunches back to the dingy cubbies.

That was more punishment than even I could stand, so I decided to call it a day. "How long have you been in here?" I asked Ms. Hackett.

"Two days," she said. "It could last a month." She was somber at the prospect. "I regret doing it but with Christmas coming, they were extra excitable."

"Well, good luck," I told her.

DECEMBER 16

There were a lot of cars in the parking lot for the December Save Our Students meeting. The only spot left was beside an enormous puddle. The puddle was more of a pond, actually. It was about eight by sixteen feet and was filled with murky water. I ended up parking down the street and hiking back to school.

Mr. Martin chased me down the hall and asked me to substitute for a couple of days in Ms. Singh's room. I couldn't say "no" to someone so needy, so I agreed.

Outside the Save Our Students meeting, I was greeted by a woman in a red Christmas sweater who handed me a candy cane. I put on a nametag and collected an agenda by the front door. I had never seen so many people in S.O.S. before, and the turnout was partially due to the splendid buffet. A long table held grits, eggs, sausage, fruit, and cinnamon rolls.

We filled our plates, and the S.O.S. director introduced the guest speaker, Judge Wilcox from a neighboring county, who told us about his educational programs. "I never just wanted to put people in jail," the judge said, "so I started programs for kids." He told us about hosting field trips at the county courthouse. Students toured the facilities and saw the courtrooms, the law library, and the judge's chambers. Lawyers guided students around in small groups. Individual students could also shadow court employees such as bailiffs, court reporters, and even the judge, himself. "We're giving them career options," the judge explained. "And if students can't come to the courthouse, we go to their schools."

Students could also attend carefully selected trials. "It's important for them to see that Judge Judy is not real," the judge said. "Those clowns on TV are not real. It's totally, totally distorted."

The judge reserved the very front row of the courtroom for school groups. "We take safeguards so they won't see inappropriate cases," he said. "We wouldn't want anyone seeing a relative."

I mentally applauded the judge's efforts to expose kids to various professions and combat stereotypes. The meeting went downhill from there, though.

Judge Wilcox showed a videotape from his public video library. A variety of tapes were available for checkout, including ones on defensive driving and teenage pregnancy. He told us some of the tapes had even won Emmy awards.

The tape featured an adolescent boot camp. The judge proudly told us that he showed it at a community meeting, recently, and several members had requested copies. We watched kids, in the video, as they were stripped down, sprayed with chemicals to fight lice, and shoved behind razor wire. The narrator described the grim daily regime: grueling jogs, long workdays, bad food, and solitary confinement. "If you use a gun in a crime," said the narrator, "you skip boot camp and go straight to prison."

We watched a frightened-looking middle school group visit the boot camp on a field trip. The school group watched several guards gang up on an prisoner and make him cry.

I looked around to gauge the audience reaction. A new minister in town was nodding vigorously but most people just looked grim. S.O.S. members were mostly counselors, educators, nurses, and social workers. They were people in the helping and healing professions, and intimidation was not their style. A foster father and the school's former librarian were both frowning but Ms. Wilkins's face was a mask.

Afterwards, the lively discussion I hoped for didn't ensue because the audience was afraid to argue with a judge. He gave us his phone number and received a smattering of applause before leaving.

We continued our meeting. A new minister was introduced to the group. He had just moved to town from Cincinnati and planned to start a mentoring program for high school drop-outs, similar to one he began back home. "Our program is for kids on the streets," he said, "kids that have exhausted the traditional routes like school. We help them get GEDs and construction jobs. We offer social skills and leadership classes. We have an alumni program so they can stay connected."

The director of S.O.S. jumped in. "When I talked to Reverend James on the phone," she said, "I liked his motto. It's 'We don't compete; we complete.'"

A social worker introduced another new program in the area, Great Grandparents. She passed out brochures. The program provided counseling, health care, and legal assistance to grandparents who were raising one or more grandchildren. In low-income Peachtree County, many grandparents would qualify.

The meeting ended, and I followed Ms. Wilkins to lunch. I wanted to get her take on the video.

"Boot camp is old. It's just old," she told me. "It doesn't work." She emphasized her point by sweeping her arm across the packed lunchroom. "I have a whole room, here, full of kids who've been to boot camp."

The generally upbeat counselor wore a deep frown and was definitely having a bad day. "I've been here ten years," she said, "and I've never seen so many conduct disordered students in my life! CD, ODD, whatever you call it. I call it B-A-D." I knew we had reached a low point when a woman who hated labeling, stooped to labeling, herself.

I visited Mr. Owens's room to find him excited about a new, ten-part documentary on the twentieth century. "We watched the seventies, yesterday, and today we're going to watch the eighties," he said.

Danita helped promote the film by saying she liked it. "What exactly did you like?" asked Mr. Owens.

"The stuff about Watergate," said Danita. I did a quick headcount, and there were only eight kids in the room.

"They didn't know what a mushroom cloud was!" Mr. Owens told me, amazed. "I couldn't believe it. I was so afraid of them." He turned to a boy. "Remember, when you asked me what a mushroom cloud was?

"I used to work on a nuclear submarine," Mr. Owens told students. "We had missiles on my sub." He drew a missile on the board. "Just one of our warheads was 500 times bigger than those dropped on Japan. Each sub had sixteen missiles, and there were forty-one subs. We had enough power to destroy the world eleven times over.

"I want you to understand," he told students, "that nuclear war *really* scared people."

"I couldn't work on a submarine," a boy said. "I'd get claustrophobia."

"It wasn't that bad," Mr. Owens told him. "It stank, though." He pointed to the ceiling. "If you dropped that ceiling and halved this room and covered the windows, that's what it would be like. Plus the floor would have to rock."

He wheeled in a television and handed me the box cover for the eighties video. I scanned the box. Topics included Chernobyl, AIDS, Mount St. Helens, and Ronald Reagan. "I've never gotten to the eighties in history, before," Mr. Owens said. I knew it was a marvel. American history textbooks tended to be so huge that teachers hardly ever made it to the end.

"I'm glad I found these films. A lot of these topics are on the high school exit exam. See?" He showed me some pages from a study guide he'd purchased. "I can't believe I found something that covers all these topics. It's good review."

We watched the film, at least a handful of us did. We listened to eighties music and watched a lone Chinese man face down a tank in Tiananmen Square. Danita and Sugar played on a computer, as a section of the Berlin Wall came crashing down, and several boys slept. I reminded, myself, that in this school, sometimes the best you could do was teach a handful of students. Still, the limited audience was depressing.

A girl rooted around for peppermints in a pink plastic purse, and sounds of chaos blasted through the wall from Mr. Wilson's room.

After the video, Mr. Owens sat on a stool and led a discussion. Students participated, eagerly, so they had soaked up more than I thought. Mr. Owens talked about Ronald Reagan. "I was kind of surprised they were so negative about him. I remember being confused by Reagan. There were cover-ups, paper being shredded. They called him 'The Teflon President' because nothing stuck to him.

"Here's what I'd like you to think about . . . the strengths and weaknesses of all the presidents. Jimmy Carter stank as a president but now he builds homes for poor people. He's a great humanitarian. I'd like to shake his hand, now.

"Recognize that presidents are human beings," Mr. Owens told the students. "Just like if we can recognize our own strengths and weaknesses, we're better people."

He put away his stool, and we killed a few more minutes before lunch. A boy ruffled through the pink purse for candy, and Mr. Owens laughed. "I'm sorry," he told the boy, "but the image of you with that purse just cracks me up."

He teased a girl about her driving. "I don't want to be anywhere near you when you get your driver's license."

"I'm a good driver. I only hit one mailbox," the girl said, seriously. She grinned at Mr. Owens. "Anyway, you're not so hot. It can't be that hard to steer a submarine. There's nothing out there to hit."

"There's plenty to hit," said Mr. Owens, "rocks, whales, the bottom."

At lunch, I joined him and Mr. Wilson and munched on my diet meal bar that tasted like cardboard. I tried to get permission from the math teacher to revisit his classroom. I'd been there once, in the fall. He gave me the brush off, though, which I found suspicious. "We're just doing testing for the rest of the week," he said brusquely. "You won't see anything."

I changed the subject. "I hear you're getting a part-time assistant principal."

Ms. Henderson had recently confiscated several knives from students and had emphasized the school's weapon problem to the board of education. The board became so concerned about liability that it finally hired an assistant principal to handle discipline. The new A.P. was only part-time, though.

"I guess that's good," Mr. Owens said about the part-time assistant principal. "This year, since we haven't had an A.P., I've been sending all my problem students right to Ms. Henderson. Actually, it's been kind of nice. We haven't had that interim step. There's been nothing between a warning and suspension."

He was frustrated, though, with the board's waffling, first eliminating then appointing an assistant principal. He addressed me as if I were a board member. "Just tell us what you want us to do and we'll do it," he said, loudly. "If you want us to be punitive, we will be. If you want us to be therapeutic, okay. But, please just stop jerking us around."

Next, I went to computer class where a fight was brewing. The computer teacher was there, only briefly, to discuss an assignment on the board. The assignment looked pretty interesting, to me. Students were asked to define "ethics" as it related to computer technology then name three ethical violations. Between pornography, hate speech, and bomb building websites, there was plenty to discuss, although most of those sites were filtered out of the school.

An older woman substitute was left in charge, and I kept an eye out for trouble. A boy with a toothpick in his mouth said something that irritated a boy behind him. The next thing I knew, the boy with a toothpick was in a choke hold. The pair struggled and almost knocked over a nearby computer.

The incident reminded me of dogfights in my neighborhood dog park. Whenever there was a fight at the dog park, most dogs immediately ran towards it. It was the same with alternative students. As soon as the two boys started fighting, others zeroed in. They circled up, grinning.

The principal materialized from thin air. "We need a deputy, here," she said into her radio but stepped back. "I'm not getting into that," she said about the boys who were swinging punches. The deputy broke up the fight, and he and the principal escorted the boys out.

News traveled fast and rumors spread quickly. By the time I reached fourth period English class, the fight sounded much worse than it actually was. "I heard someone was slammed on the floor," said Sugar.

The students took a practice quiz that required them to correct grammar in several paragraphs. "If we were in Grammar Town," said Ms. Bates, "there'd be commas after the third and fourth words." Her frequent jokes about Grammar Town helped to alleviate anxiety in alternative students, who generally had very poor grammar.

Two female parole officers came into English class. Both were attractive young women wearing blue jeans and black turtlenecks. They did not meet my stereotype of burly parole officers, by any means. The blonde wore a black trench coat and the brunette wore a black pea coat. They had picked up a boy from Mr. Wilson's room and had come to get one from Ms. Bates's room. Neither boy looked unhappy to be leaving with two glamorous women, and I made a mental note to check my closet for a black turtleneck to achieve a similar look.

DECEMBER 17

I was substituting for Ms. Singh's paraprofessional, and I was surprised to learn that there were only two students in Ms. Singh's special education classroom. Just two! She actually had four students but two girls were visiting the department chair's classroom. *If I couldn't handle two students then I had no business being a certified teacher.*

Ms. Singh's high school students were labeled SESD, Special Education Severe Disruption, whereas the other special education students were just labeled Learning Disabled. That was why Ms. Singh had fewer students. The woman had completed all of the coursework for a doctoral degree in special education and was ABD, "All But The Dissertation." She drove over fifty miles, every day, to work, and I was impressed that she drove that distance to teach at Peachtree Alternative School. Like so many teachers at the school, she could have easily worked somewhere else.

I gave Jarrod the note from Ashley Bryan, and he began drawing a picture for Ashley, a Christmas scene with Santa Claus. Sixteen-year-old Jarrod stamped his picture, many times, with a green Christmas stamp then asked to stamp my hand so I stuck it out.

Lunch was late for us because preschool was having a special Christmas program in the cafeteria. We weren't scheduled to eat until 12:30, and Purple Pete was pacing up and down. "I'm so hungry," he said. *That was from a boy who never, ever ate lunch.*

Jarrod wrote a poem for me, and Pete kept on pacing. Ms. Singh tried to persuade him to do some work but he refused. "I'm not doing that stuff. That's for little kids," he shouted about some worksheets, which were indeed simplistic.

A big, blonde girl named Kim came back to watch music videos on the room's one computer. Actually, it was just one music video, a rap song that she played over and over again. I noticed that Kim did not speak in a normal tone of voice. Instead, she shouted every word. She was an extremely loud girl, and I wondered if she was hard of hearing.

Our special holiday lunch was chicken fingers, macaroni and cheese, green beans, and strawberry shortcake. We gathered our trays and returned to the classroom so the custodial staff could clean the lunchroom.

Ms. Singh's student number four, a small black girl, flounced in. She was followed by the beautiful brunette parole officer, who again wore her uniform of blue jeans, black turtleneck, and black pea coat. The girl slumped in a chair and the parole officer sat across from her, striking a relaxed pose. She stretched out her long legs, crossed one booted foot over the other, and folded her hands over her stomach. "Tell me what's been going on," the parole officer told the girl.

Jarrod and I were coloring some pictures that I brought from home. We listened with our crayons poised.

The girl was a tough nut to crack and just mumbled a few responses. A kid from across the hall came over to watch the exchange. He sat atop a desk and grinned at the pair of females. One thing that was hard for me to adjust to, in special education, was the free flow of students from one room to another. They seemed to be in constant motion.

The parole officer kept trying to converse. "I hear you've been sleeping," she said to the girl. "You're not supposed to be sleeping in school. Why do you guys do that?" I flashed a guilty glance at Purple Pete who was asleep with his face on the desk. He had pulled up his sweatshirt hood, put on black leather gloves, and covered his mouth, bandit-style, with a bandana. Ms. Singh had long since left the room.

There I was coloring, while Purple Pete was sleeping. The visiting kid from across the hall kept making quips from the sidelines, which irritated the parole officer. "I can't talk in here. Come on," she ordered, and the girl slowly followed her out the door.

The next class was gym, and I dreaded going. Not only was it a terrible facility but it tended to be chaos. The alternative students had very little gym equipment beyond a few limp basketballs.

The special education classes mingled in 200 Hall before heading to the gym, and a new deputy, a tall bronze-skinned man with a dark mustache, watched us closely. He was replacing a corporal who had transferred to a new school. Prior to working at Peachtree Alternative, the new officer had worked at city hall.

While waiting, I was struck by how big some of the high school boys were. A new boy in a red parka was even bigger than Malcolm. He defied the department chair when she tried to get him to go back to class. He hadn't earned the privilege of going to the gym. The big kid loomed over the department chair, yelled profanity, and refused to budge.

The confrontation made me nervous because the department chair had already been assaulted twice that year. The kids standing near the pair scooted away. The department chair decided to drop the matter, and the big kid accompanied us to the gym, after all.

Ms. Singh proceeded us to unlock the gym. I led the line over and promptly lost the back half. "Where are the rest of the kids?" Ms. Singh asked.

"They're coming," I said, feeling frustrated. *How was I supposed to keep them from lagging behind?* Finally, the back half of the line emerged from the main building, followed by another substitute paraprofessional.

I had brought along my copy of *The New Games Book* that was filled with cooperative games with titles such as "Hug Tag," "Blob," and "Catch the Dragon's Tail." I didn't have the courage to use it, though. It would probably be a fatal attempt to restore order.

Ms. Singh and the substitute paraprofessional scooted to the top of the bleachers. I stood aimlessly on the gym floor for awhile. If the department chair was here, she'd be circulating around the room to combat chaos. She wouldn't be sitting on the bleachers. I stood for a few more minutes and then resigned myself to being unathletic and a coward. I was too bad at basketball to join the bigger kids and too wimpy to circulate. I climbed the bleachers and sat beside the other women. Warm air blasted us from a repaired overhead heater while the rest of the gym was freezing.

Ms. Pearl came in and joined us near the rafters, as did Ms. W-J, after depositing some middle school students on the gym floor. Now, there were twenty-two kids on the floor and five women in the rafters. We were really shirking our duties. I tried to at least keep a headcount of the kids, in case any of them ran away, but it wasn't easy with all the movement. It reminded of my zookeeper days, when I had to count monkeys in an enclosure to make sure none of them had escaped. The teenagers were either dribbling balls or going in and out of the men's room. Some kept disappearing into a storage closet, probably to smoke or make out.

Tomorrow was only a half day for students, if they brought a note from home. Students could leave after exams, with parental permission. "Will you take me to get some water?" a kid asked the other substitute paraprofessional, and they left the gymnasium.

I was startled from my daze. "There's no water in here?" I asked Ms. Pearl, thinking it was downright disgraceful for a public school gymnasium not to have water.

"There are water fountains," said Ms. Pearl, "but they haven't worked all year. The ones in the school taste terrible. I don't drink out of them."

I had stayed away from the fountains, myself, which spewed brown water. I went over and checked the gym water fountains to confirm that they were indeed broken.

The substitute paraprofessional returned and climbed back up the bleachers. She pulled the back of her jacket up over her head and went right to sleep. I couldn't believe she was sleeping. I, myself, was sitting but at least I was watching. I barely resisted tapping the woman on the shoulder and giving her a lecture.

It was Kim's birthday, and the teachers gave the big, blonde girl a present. "Y'all are so sweet," Kim gushed as she pulled some makeup from a gift bag. It was the first time I'd heard her speak without shouting. Thankfully, no one plunged us into darkness, and we stayed in the gym until 2:45.

The big scary kid in the red parka stopped by Ms. Singh's room and announced, to thin air, that he was walking home. He left quickly, and I hurried to bus duty.

Outside, we stamped around in the cold. "We had problems out here, last week," Mr. Martin told me, "so we need plenty of teachers." I waited with the kids for the special education buses to arrive. Students were rowdy and shoved each other. A female deputy from the sheriff's department arrived for added security. A girl made a face at the deputy, and the deputy made one back. The woman should have known better. *Don't retaliate,* I wanted to tell her.

The special education students piled into two buses. "Where is Tyler?" a bus driver asked about the big boy in the red parka.

"He's not here?" Ms. Pearl looked around.

"He said he was walking home," I told the women.

"What? He's not supposed to walk home! He rides the bus!" said Ms. Pearl, frowning at me but how could I have stopped such a big, defiant kid? It irritated me that so much of special education at Peachtree Alternative was just keeping track of students.

"I'll go call his mother," Mr. Martin said.

Ms. Pearl wanted the students to leave early, tomorrow, as much as anyone. She even followed the buses and shouted, "Remember to bring your permission forms," as they pulled away.

DECEMBER 18

The academic counselor had the unfortunate task of supervising standardized testing, and she raced around the cafeteria with a heavy stack of papers and a pencil behind her ear. Even the special ed alternative students had to take standardized tests. "Who is Ms. Singh's parapro?" she asked.

"That would be me," I said, raising my hand, and Ms. Wilkins explained how to fill out the answer sheets.

"Make sure you write everything in pencil," she told me. I took the stack of papers and waited for breakfast to end. Across the cafeteria, a boy lobbed his milk cartoon at another student.

At the teachers' table, I learned that, over the weekend, a student was caught carrying a gun. He claimed to have found the gun, and the police must have believed him because he was in school rather than jail. "I hope it wasn't used to kill anyone," said Ms. Pearl.

The special education department chair sat with students and ate a muffin. She was trying to keep the peace, and when she saw Andrew, the trashcan thrower, aim a punch at another student, she reminded him to take his medicine.

In Ms. Singh's classroom, Jarrod sat inside a cubby, Purple Pete sat by the window, and Kim flitted about the room. The department chair dropped off the big, defiant kid who'd gone AWOL on Thursday, and he hunkered down in a desk. He shoved his standardized test off the desk, tossed a few balls of paper at Kim, and then laid his head down, quietly. In the silence, I did some origami, folding squares of colored paper into small figures. I was trying to follow Ms. Hackett's example and role model industriousness.

"You have to take your test," Ms. Singh told the big, defiant kid and his response shocked me.

He leapt from his seat, clenching a pencil in his fist and raising it overhead. "I'm going to stab this pencil in your forehead!" he shouted. To me, it was no idle threat but Ms. Singh just ignored him. There was irony to the biggest boy in school threatening the smallest teacher and, in that case, I thought making someone take a standardized test wasn't worth the risk.

Kim took her test and so did Pete. Ms. Singh gave Jarrod a distracting math assignment and he gave it a try. He kept shouting out answers, though, and I hurried to keep him quiet during testing. Looking at his math paper, I realized that Jarrod couldn't comprehend any of the questions, and when I told him to write a number, he wrote down something completely different.

Ms. Singh left the room to deliver the completed tests, and the big boy perked up. He banged on his desk and yawned dramatically. For some unknown reason, Kim decided to go over and sit in his lap. She put an arm around the boy and rubbed his shoulder. *Of all the unappealing boys!* Girls at Peachtree Alternative were always draping themselves over boys. It was their way of seeking attention. Many of the girls at Peachtree Alternative were promiscuous, and many were victims of sexual abuse.

"Ooo, look at them!" Jarrod said but I decided to ignore it. I was not going to risk being stabbed with a pencil. I started to read *The Best Christmas Pageant Ever* aloud to Jarrod, reminding myself that sometimes the best you could do was help one kid. He rested his head on my shoulder, as the volume in the classroom started to rise. Ms. Singh was taking her own sweet time in returning.

The three other students were now over by the computer watching music videos. Kim was shouting about her brother's being in jail for statutory rape. Her shouting was jarring, and I wanted to shake Jarrod's head off my shoulder but resisted. He probably didn't get much attention at home. I raised my reading voice, in order to be heard over the din, and wondered if the severely disabled teenager could follow the story.

Ms. Singh came back and sent Kim and her friend across the hall. She asked me to work with Pete on his reading while she worked with Jarrod. "He can't read," she whispered about Pete. "You have to read aloud then ask him questions." She pointed to a set of thought questions at the end of a chapter.

Pete and I began reading a boring excerpt from a textbook about a girl who aspired to be an artist. Pete struggled, mightily, to read aloud, and I helped him by pronouncing words. "I understand them," he told me. "I just can't say them."

"You're doing well," I said, pleased that he was trying so hard. We made it to the end of the chapter, and I started asking Pete the thought questions.

He had paid more attention than I did and had no trouble responding. "Nice job," I told him.

Pete had a lot to say, now that we had bonded. He regaled me with stories from his life in New York and the gang he used to be a part of. I had no doubt that he was speaking the truth but I didn't need to hear it and didn't want to encourage his bragging about gangs. I tried to change the subject but he kept on talking.

It was hard to squelch Pete's stream of talk. He wouldn't stop, even as I went to help Jarrod with his work. Finally, he resorted to drawing gang symbols on the board.

After a morning of standardized testing, the high school had emptied but plenty of special education students remained because they failed to bring signed permission forms from home. Pete left but Kim and Jarrod stayed in school, and another boy from the department chair's room joined us. He and Kim found a huge tub of glitter and dumped it on the carpet, while my back was turned. They made the mess worse by sprinkling it all over themselves. The glitter was ground into the carpet and would have to be vacuumed.

I colored some diagrams, and Jarrod babbled at me so relentlessly that I thought I'd go crazy. He would not be quiet for a second, and none of his talk made any sense. It was almost a form of torture. I put a stop to it by reading aloud a second book. We'd already finished *The Best Christmas Pageant Ever* so I began the sequel.

I thought Jarrod liked the books because they featured some really bad kids called the Horrible Herdmans who created chaos. The Herdmans could easily be kids at Peachtree Alternative School.

Jarrod interrupted me to say that, last night, he attended the funeral of a boy who committed suicide. "He ran in front of a truck, on purpose," Jarrod said.

"I'm sorry," I said. That day, alone, I'd heard stories of gangs, jail, and suicide.

I kept on reading, and Jarrod started an art project where he covered a piece of paper with a lot of staples. He and I stayed in the classroom while Ms. Singh and some other kids went to the gym.

I had gone through my entire substitute teacher survival kit. I'd done the origami, the tangram puzzles, and pages from a coloring book. I'd read one and a half chapter books. More than one veteran teacher had told me, "You can never plan too much," and, boy, were they right.

Chapter 6

January

JANUARY 7

It was the first day of a new semester, and I started off in Ms. Bates's ninth grade English class. As usual in the mornings, she played soft classical music. Five black boys sat on one side of the room. Four of them were familiar but one was new. Rick Wilson, whose parent conference I'd attended, wore another droopy plaid shirt and sat alone on the other side of the room. All of the boys wore baggy jeans and high-top sneakers.

"Hey, lady, you can't teach five African Americans something they don't already know," the new boy yelled at Ms. Bates, but she ignored him.

The counselor stepped in with Ms. Bates's new lists of students for the semester. She wore a black sweater, a silver necklace, and a tinkling charm bracelet. Ms. Wilkins had once told me that she wore black when she wanted to feel powerful and pastels when she wanted to have fun.

We stood for the pledge of allegiance but the boys talked during the moment of silence, which annoyed Ms. Bates. She moved to the front of the room. "There's going to be some changes, this semester," she told students. "If you don't pull your pants up, it's no longer a dress code violation. It's willful refusal, the first time; insubordination, the second; then failure to obey." The boys groaned.

"No headphones are allowed. We'll lock them up if we find them. If you sleep in class, we'll ask you to sit up no more than twice." She outlined the subsequent consequences, which were calling a parent, lunch detention, and then suspension. *Good luck with all that,* I thought.

"A reason a lot of you didn't pass, last semester, was you didn't do the work," said Ms. Bates. "When I was cleaning out folders, I found some work that wasn't even handed in. Be sure to hand things in.

Figure 6. Cracked Track with Weeds.

"If you didn't write in your journal, it really hurt your grade. It's an easy A, and it can really make a difference in your final grade. I expect a minimum of five sentences per day."

Ms. Bates popped in a video about the origins of the English language and handed out an accompanying set of questions. A talking head told us that the first symbol of the alphabet, in most languages, was the letter A because the "ah" sound was the universal sound of satisfaction after a good meal or sex. None of the boys reacted so the comment had escaped them.

Afterwards, Ms. Bates perched on a stool and reviewed answers. She had trouble understanding what the boys were saying because they mumbled so badly. She cocked her head slightly and looked confused.

The boys didn't always understand her, either. One boy asked if they could do family trees, that semester. "I need to figure out how to make it relevant to class," Ms. Bates said.

"I didn't get none of that," the boy told her, and she clarified.

The students would have to read two books that semester: one from the Peachtree County reading list and one that they chose, themselves. Ms. Bates would give them thirty minutes, each day, for silent reading.

Towards the end of session, Ms. Bates said, "Tell me one thing you learned from the video." She went around the room, and all the boys but one could provide an answer.

"Just say something, man!" a classmate told the struggling student.

"He's thinking," Ms. Bates said, looking hopeful, but Rick Wilson just sat in his droopy plaid shirt and didn't answer.

Eight of the ten students in Mr. Owens's American history class were new. The agenda on the board read "Introductions, Rules, Procedures, Interest Inventory, Pre-Test." Mr. Owens introduced himself and said the students could ask him questions, provided they were serious.

He gave them an incentive. "If you ask good questions, we might not even get to the pre-test this morning."

A redheaded girl, in front, went first and asked an odd question. "Have you ever been in a car wreck?"

Mr. Owens responded with surprising frankness. He told a cautionary tale about the time he received a DUI. "There was ice on the road, and I shouldn't have been drinking and driving, in the first place. I lost control and my car went upside down, over a cliff. I was thrown twenty feet.

"I totaled my wife's car. I was an EMT, at the time, and the guys that came to rescue me were my buddies. It was embarrassing. I had to do all kinds of things to make amends: pay a fine, take driving classes, do community service. It was an expensive drink, I'll tell you—a $30,000 screwdriver."

There were no other questions so Mr. Owens explained his grading policy. Thirty percent of a student's grade was behavior/attendance and seventy percent was coursework. "Please be here. If you're absent, please ask for makeup work." He paused then gave students a much-needed compliment. "I'm proud of you already. I'm fiercely proud." He looked around the room. "Some of you had me last period for science. In this class, I'll tell more stories. We'll watch more movies. My American history class is my most casual class," he said, and the students weren't disappointed by the news.

"We'll take a lot of notes. If you're not used to taking notes, let me know so I can help you. If you take really good notes, you can use them on your tests." It was a tremendous incentive. "That's what notes are for," said Mr. Owens. "I'm not asking you to memorize the Constitution."

"Do we have to learn about wars and presidents?" asked the redheaded girl.

"There's more to American history than wars," said Mr. Owens.

He told them more about memorization. He tended to memorize a lot of things, himself, just because he liked to. "My wife knows I have a lot of stuff crammed in my head." He tapped his forehead and laughed. "I'll blow you away with all the crap that I have in here. It's just stupid stuff . . . factoids.

"But I'm not going to force you to memorize dates. Knowing that the Battle of Shiloh was in 1862 won't get you very far in life." *I wished I had a*

history teacher like him when I was in high school, someone down-to-earth,
who let you use your notes on tests and didn't make you memorize.

"We may have debates, in here. I may ask you to debate something you're morally against but it's a good way to learn about something."

"That sounds fun," said the redheaded girl.

"Is the Civil War coming first?" asked a boy named Bill, who had been retained from last semester. In fact, it was Bill's second year at Peachtree Alternative School.

"No, because it didn't come first."

"What did?"

"Native Americans," said Mr. Owens.

"I don't want to learn about them," said Bill.

"Too bad," said his teacher.

Mr. Owens indicated the space around his desk. "That's the forbidden zone. There's a force field around it," he said, and students laughed. "If I find you back there, it's like finding someone in a bank vault. Please respect my privacy."

The subject of privacy sparked Bill to ask a question. "What makes you want to search someone?" he asked Mr. Owens.

"If I have reasonable cause."

"I don't think we should have searches," said Bill.

"Well, there are a lot of court cases dealing with students' rights. We'll go over them. Both Deputy Rodriguez and I believe in students' rights."

"I'm for and against searches," said a blonde boy. "I don't want anybody searching me but I don't want someone bringing a gun to school."

"Remember," Bill told Mr. Owens, "how, last year, the boys kept getting put in that room, while the girls were being searched."

"The girls were searched a lot, last year," Mr. Owens agreed. "We're short-staffed, here, and we have to wear a lot of hats. During fourth period, my free period, I have to be a teacher *and* an administrator. I have to break up fights, treat medical emergencies, do searches.

"I don't mind searching middle schoolers, as much, because I don't know them. They're not my students but I'd be very self-conscious searching you.

"Please don't get into trouble," he told students. "I don't mind being your teacher but I *hate* being involved when there's bad news. When cops are here to get you because of drugs, I *hate* that. That's between you and the legal system. I'm not an administrator. I don't want to be an administrator. I want to be a teacher.

"Please don't make it uncomfortable for us," said Mr. Owens. "Let me know, ahead of time, so I don't have to get involved and don't have to be embarrassed. If you accidentally bring a lighter to school, hand it over. I've held a pack of cigarettes, before. I won't do it every day, though.

"Every day, try to make it through class. Be straight with me, and I'll be straight with you."

His rationale, discomfort at having to do searches, was a convincing reason not to bring drugs and weapons to school. Mr. Owens elaborated on his expectations for student behavior. "I don't want you sleeping but if you tell me you have a splitting headache, I'll understand. Just let me know. Any sort of relationship problems you're having that will interfere with work—parent: child, boyfriend:girlfriend—you have to communicate it with me."

He went over his pet peeves. On the board, he wrote, "Saying 'shut up', Whining, Interrupting, Asking twice." A reason Mr. Owens didn't like whining was he used to be a veterinary technician. *Was there nothing the man hadn't done?* He had been a vet tech for ten years. In Florida, he told us, he would see dogs that had been chewed by alligators but were still wagging their tails. "I came to respect those animals, their strength and fortitude." The dogs that irritated him, though, were "little dogs named Fifi that screamed about shots.

"Over the years, that has spread throughout my body." He shivered dramatically. He was a dramatic guy who punctuated his stories with sweeping gestures. "I don't like whining from dogs, and I don't like whining from people, especially grownups."

"Look." He held up a bumper sticker. "I even made a bumper sticker that I took to a Libertarian convention. It says, 'Stop whining. Work harder'."

"Another of my pet peeves is asking twice. I used to work for a breeder of German shepherds in New Hampshire. Those dogs could sit on command. I think if a German shepherd puppy can sit, right away, people can, too." The kids looked around and grinned.

He gave students a few minutes to fill out questionnaires about themselves. "If you're going to be silly on this, I'll see straight through it," he warned. "Be serious. Don't mess with me or I'll psychoanalyze you. I'm an amateur psychologist."

Mr. Owens, as a teacher, was easy-going and eccentric. Even his threats were original. Between Civil War reenacting, serving on a submarine, being an emergency medical technician, and working with dogs, he was cool, to boot.

He scanned questionnaires, as they were handed in. The first question was about student strengths and weaknesses. "Does anyone want to share what they wrote?"

"My weakness," said the redheaded girl, "is being too compassionate."

"That's cool," said Mr. Owens and revealed his own weaknesses. "I have a reputation for being cold and not showing emotions."

Bill rose to his defense. "But you're one of the calmest teachers, here, because you were on a submarine and you had to be calm."

Mr. Owens laughed at that. "If I was up here all hyper," he told the students, "you guys would stress out."

Mr. Owens returned to his strengths and weaknesses. "My strength is being quiet and my weakness is being quiet. I got a B in one of my graduate classes, last semester, because I didn't speak up enough. It's the first B I've gotten since the '80s but, at this stage in life, I don't really care."

He read aloud some of his own answers to the questionnaire. "This will be earth-shattering," he announced. "My favorite subject is U.S. history. I've had a lifelong interest in it, fostered by my parents. I remember going past Stone Mountain and wondering about those men carved on it. I remember loving the cyclorama, in Atlanta, with the Civil War painting that wraps around."

Mr. Owen read another question. "What do I like to do in my spare time?" he asked. "I like to spend time with my family."

"You like to show off your car," said Bill.

"I do not." Mr. Owens corrected him. "I like to *tinker* with my car. I like to do Civil War and World War II reenacting. I've got a World War II reenactment coming up in Florida. We'll crawl around the palmettos and be bitten by chiggers."

"Is it like paintball?" asked the redheaded girl.

"Sort of."

"Do you use real bullets?" she asked.

"Real cartridges. It's loud. It's grown men playing cowboys and Indians except with very expensive equipment like airplanes. We have B52 bombers flying overhead. A B24 bomber flew over, one time, at treetop level. It scared me to death. I didn't know they could do that."

"How do you know if you're dead?" someone asked.

"You take a guess. If you're running through the woods, and someone stands up, aims a gun at you, and pulls the trigger, you can be pretty sure you're dead. If you're shot, you take off your hat.

"I do reconnaissance, now," he said. "I go and find out what the enemy is doing."

"They reenact all kinds of wars," Bill told the other students. "I'd like to see one."

"I will not do Germans," Mr. Owens said. "It doesn't sit well with me. And I won't reenact Vietnam for moral reasons.

"I've had a grenade dropped in my lap during reenacting. That's not good, either. Most of the time we do scenarios, like go rescue an American pilot who crashed behind enemy lines.

"In Civil War reenacting, six hour battles are condensed into one. In the movies *Gods and Generals* and *Andersonville,* they recruited reenactors who already had the equipment. In *Andersonville,* I was a Yankee prisoner, slogging around and being treated like dirt. I told my friend Bob, 'Stick with me, Buddy, and I'll get you on film.' He was in the movie six or seven times but they cut me out of everything!"

"Can we watch that in here?" a boy asked.

"Yes, when we get to that topic."

"What kind of guns do you have?"

"I have a N44 carbiner with a bayonet," Mr. Owens told them. "I don't have live ammo in the house. I have a gun for Civil War reenacting and one for World War II reenacting . . . And, no, I don't use them for protection. If someone broke into my house, do you think he'd wait thirty seconds while I loaded my gun?"

Mr. Owens pretended to talk to a burglar. "Now, just stand there, buddy. You're going to be real sorry, in just a minute." He pantomimed fumbling with a gun, and students laughed.

"All right, y'all," Mr. Owens concluded, and the class let out a collective sigh of satisfaction. It was an audible sound of a good period. Students were also stretching and smiling.

During lunch, Ms. Bates told the other teachers, "It's been a good day, so far. I thought it would take awhile for them to settle down, after the break, but that hasn't been the case." Mr. Owens and the math teacher said their classes had been good, too.

"By golly, I'm going to have one whole day that's good," Ms. Bates declared. "I don't care what the rest of the semester is like. Today is going to be great."

The math teacher bragged that he only had two students in his fourth period class, and Mr. Owens told him, "I'm going to knock you out of that chair. My smallest class has ten students."

"What happened to Mike?" the math teacher asked about the troublemaker, who wore yellow, from last semester.

"He went to youth detention," said Ms. Bates. "He didn't pass his drug test so he violated parole."

I passed the principal on my way to computer class. "How was your Christmas?" I asked her.

"Good," she said, "but I started getting antsy during the last three days. I was ready to come back here, believe it or not. I don't know what I'm going to do with myself when I retire."

JANUARY 15

The special education department chair spotted me in the hall and asked if I wouldn't mind substituting for her in the afternoon. "They don't have anybody to be an administrator so I'm going to do it," she told me. Ms. Henderson and the new assistant principal were in meetings, and Ms. Wilkins had the flu. I agreed to substitute for the special ed department chair while she subbed for the principal.

"Are you sure you'll be all right?" the woman asked.

"I'll be fine," I said, blithely.

She turned the class over to me right away, and I was thrust into teacher mode with Ms. Pearl as my paraprofessional. The department chair departed too quickly, as far as I was concerned, and I was left standing with a physics textbook in my hand. I didn't even have my substitute teaching kit. The special education students had a physics assignment to complete. They were supposed to read a chapter then answer some thought questions. They were scheduled to go outside for free time, come back in for another assignment, and then attend a Black History Month program in the library.

Ms. Pearl prompted me. "James knows the definition of 'mechanical energy'," she said.

I asked James for the definition, and he told me then slammed his book shut. "I ain't doing no more fucking work," he announced. Some kids copied from each other right under my nose. I loomed over them but it didn't stop the copying. Ms. Pearl collected the papers, and it was time to escape outdoors.

"Kenneth and Kenya have to stay in an extra ten minutes before free time," Ms. Pearl told me. "Do you want to stay or should I?"

"I'll stay," I blurted, thinking I could easily handle a pair of students.

The kids were awful while we waited in the room. They wrestled, kept slamming the door, and decided to make phone calls on the department chair's telephone. I tried to stop them from all three activities, in vain. "Time to go," I announced, well before our time was up.

"But it hasn't been ten minutes," said the boy.

"It doesn't matter. We're going."

I had no idea where we were going so I followed the pair down 200 Hall. Kenneth pounded on the doors of other classrooms and made faces in the windows until I patted his back. I was hesitant to touch potentially explosive kids but I knew that pats on the back and shoulders were fairly acceptable. I followed my charges out a door and around to the back of the building. An old track and field were filled with weeds.

It was a relief to spot Ms. Pearl and Ms. Singh propped against some playground equipment. Jarrod was swinging so high that the beams creaked ominously.

Ms. Singh asked the standard question of a sub. "Who are you, today?"

"Ms. Kelley," I told her.

It was nice to be in the fresh air, instead of inside the crumbling building. Down the road, the old school administration building, which was built at roughly the same time as Peachtree Alternative School, was slowly being evacuated because employees were becoming mysteriously ill. The superintendent had referred to the old administrative building as "the sick building." Whether it was lead paint, asbestos, or rodent droppings, something was not right, and it made me worry more about our own building.

All of the kids except Jarrod were walking laps around the cracked track. A new girl in Ms. Singh's class kicked her wooden clogs off and they sailed through the air. They would really hurt if they hit someone. Wooden clogs were common when I was in college, and we were actually taught that they could be used as self-defense weapons. "Stop that!" Ms. Singh yelled at the girl kicking her clogs.

"Why?" the girl snarled. "They're *my* shoes."

"They can hurt somebody. That's why," said Ms. Singh but the girl put them on and did it again.

Ms. Pearl went inside to warm up, and Ms. Singh tried to stop a clump of kids from smoking. I sat in a swing beside Jarrod who told me he had to go to a children's hospital, next year, for a brain operation. Part of his brain damage was the result of being struck from behind by an unknown assailant at a gas station.

"I'm sorry, honey. I'll say a prayer for you," I told him.

Kenneth was in the bushes throwing rocks at a group of neighborhood men. "Stop that, Kenneth!" Ms. Singh shouted.

"Stop what?" he asked, innocently.

"Stop throwing rocks!" It is too late, though, because he had antagonized a gang. Three angry men headed our way, and my heart started pounding. One of them had a disability, himself, a limp left arm that hung at an awkward angle.

"Can't you control these kids?" the man yelled at us adults.

Fortunately, Ms. Pearl had just returned. "Who threw the rocks?" she asked, and I was grateful for her intervention.

"Kenneth," I told her.

"I did not!" says Kenneth, and he and a buddy made things worse by hurling insults at the men.

"Be quiet!" Ms. Pearl yelled at them. She turned to the men. "I'm sorry. I'll take care of it," she told them. She escorted the two boys to the principal's office, and the men returned to their street corner.

"This is why we don't like to bring them out here," Ms. Singh told me. "They smoke or harass people. At least we can contain them in the gym." *And I thought being in the gym was an all-time low but, no, there were even worse scenarios.*

Jarrod watched the rock throwers leave. "Let's say a prayer for them," he said to me. "You go first."

I bowed my head. "Dear God, please help these children live happy and productive lives."

"Amen," said Jarrod.

The new girl in clogs had decided, on her own, that it was time to go in. "Stop! Where are you going?" yelled Ms. Singh but the new girl led the rest of the kids inside. We had no choice but to follow. That, more than anything, made me feel like a pawn, and I grumbled about letting a teenager dictate our schedule. Our discipline of the students was downright abysmal.

The department chair had forgotten to leave our next assignment, and I worried about having nothing to do until the Black History Month activity in the library. I didn't even attempt to improvise seatwork. In desperation, I pulled two good books off the shelf, Louis Sachar's *Holes* and Christopher Paul Curtis's *The Watsons Go to Birmingham—1963.*

"I'm going to read aloud," I announced, showing them both covers. "Pick one or I'll choose." Giving students just two things to choose from was a standard classroom management technique. It gave students some freedom of choice but facilitated compliance.

The alternative kids said nothing so I chose *Holes,* whose author was renowned for his quirky sense of humor. I started to read aloud with gusto. A girl listened for about two minutes then asked if she could read aloud. "Sure," I said, handing her the book. I watched her struggle to read aloud and helped her pronounce a few words. She read several pages before losing interest and wandering off. In fact, all of the kids had wandered away while we were reading. They were out in the hall and in doorways of other classrooms.

Deputy Rodriguez arrived and herded kids back inside my room, and I was embarrassed to have literally lost them. When a majority of kids returned, I closed the door, trapping them, and kept on reading. It was the only thing I knew to do. I raised my voice over students' chatter, and out of the corner of my eye, I spotted a kid remove a pack of cigarettes from his pocket. For a moment, I really wanted to throw up my hands and walk out of the building. Instead, I confiscated the cigarettes.

Only one kid actually listened to me, and he quoted a couple of lines before I even reached them. He knew the book by heart. It was an appropriate book for alternative schoolers. The main character, Stanley, was in trouble with the law, as were most of the students in the room. Stanley was sent off to work camp, and local at-risk kids were sent to Peachtree Alternative School. They could relate, if they would only listen.

I told myself that at least I was reaching one kid, until even he stopped listening. Mr. Martin came in to use the department chair's phone and gave me a sympathetic look. I kept on reading to the air, hoping that something was sinking in. I wanted to at least appear to be trying. Ms. Singh's paraprofessional also dropped by and gave me her typical big hug as I perched on a stool with an open book.

"No one is listening to you read!" a boy shouted at me, and his mean tone hurt. I knew you weren't supposed to retaliate but I lost it and snapped back.

"I don't care if you're listening or not," I told him. "I like to read aloud." I read three whole chapters to myself, while seven students huddled in a back row. I thought that, at least, they were great chapters.

I poked my head into the hall. "Don't we have a program in the library?" I asked other teachers, in desperation. Ms. Singh hadn't heard of one and neither had Mr. Martin. Ms. Pearl came back from wherever she'd been and helped me direct students. She sent most of them to the gymnasium but a few to the library.

Kenneth didn't want to go to the library with Ms. Pearl. He threw a tantrum by swearing, throwing books, and ripping paper off the walls while I stayed out of the way.

Finally, when he calmed down, we herded a small, belligerent group to the library. Ms. Pearl popped in a film about Rosa Parks. Jarrod and I watched, while Kenneth and some other boys slept and a girl played a piano. Ms. Pearl told her to stop, and she resorted to plunking a few keys.

Kenneth just up and walked out, and Ms. Pearl pursued him. She came back alone and sat and blew her nose into a tissue. The woman was crying. She made a couple of trips to the closet where she dabbed her eyes in private. She blew her nose, again, and my hackles rose. The kids had been so bad and, probably, I had been so inept that the former navy communications specialist was crying!

I watched a greater struggle, a fight for civil rights, depicted on the screen. Finally, the school buses arrived, and the students began to leave. The girl at the piano was pretending to sleep. "Time to go," I said but she didn't move, although I was sure she heard me. At that point, I didn't care if she missed her ride home. My own rotten afternoon was almost over, and it had been a roller coaster. I'd run through a gamut of emotions. My excitement at having an assignment in the building had quickly turned to frustration. My sadness at Jarrod's terrible history and uncertain future had turned to anger at Kenneth for almost starting a gang fight. That was followed by more frustration back in the classroom and library. It was an exhausting afternoon.

"Is she coming?" Ms. Pearl asked from the library doorway.

"She heard me," I said, unkindly. I'd had my fill of misbehavior. Probably, the most admirable thing alternative teachers did, all day long, was maintain their tempers. I lost mine, hours ago.

I did bus duty and watched the alternative students be rude to a bus driver. They pushed her and swore at her. *You would think they'd be nicer to some-one who held their lives in her hands, day in and day out.*

Ms. Singh spotted me in the hall and said, "You had a bad day, today, didn't you?"

"I've had better," I grumbled.

In the department chair's room, I picked up trash and lined up chairs. Mr. Martin came in to use the phone. "How was your day?" he asked.

"Not easy," I confessed.

"They're tough kids," he reminded me.

Chapter 7

February

FEBRUARY 17

In a Save Our Students meeting, a social worker from Child Protective Services stood at a podium and told us some sobering news. In Peachtree County, caseworkers' loads had increased by 295% in the past three years, and the increase was the highest in the state. Three years ago, CPS in Peachtree County had only one supervisor and five staff members. That number had risen to three supervisors and twenty staff members. Still, the agency was understaffed and could barely meet the demand.

Why had caseloads increased so dramatically? The social worker attributed the increase to the burgeoning population in Peachtree County. The county was now considered part of a growing metropolitan area. Also, there had been some policy changes, and even referrals coming from other counties had to be investigated, if the alleged victims lived in Peachtree County. The social worker also speculated that media coverage of child abuse had led to more people to report their suspicions.

"There are a lot of false allegations," a man pointed out.

"But you can't risk ignoring them," said a woman, beside me.

A foster father tried to elaborate on the extent of child abuse in the county. Many of his foster children were former victims. "You can't understand how bad it is until you hear their stories," he said. "If we don't deal with child abuse, kids will go out there and commit crimes. Many girls do it just to get out of abusive situations."

"How can we help?" someone asked the woman at the podium.

The social worker suggested that lobbying legislators for more funding might make a difference. "Prevention is the key. We need to put more

Figure 7. An Abandoned Building in the Neighborhood.

money up front to prevent problems down the road." I suspected that everyone in the room subscribed to that philosophy. Pay for early childhood education to prevent remediation down the road. Pay for preventive health care rather than having to treat disease and drug prevention education rather than rehabilitation.

"We have to beg our legislators, pray for our legislators," the social worker continued. She turned to the Save Our Students director. "Thanks to S.O.S. for keeping us posted on legislative initiatives."

"Whenever you talk with legislators, say 'prevention, prevention,'" the director advised us.

The social worker wrapped up her presentation. "There is such a dire need. People in our agency are working around the clock, just as hard as we can."

Others were working equally hard, including teachers at Peachtree Alternative School. The teen health educator, in the county, was on the verge of losing her job unless the health department came up with more grant money. Parole officers also had heavy case loads. Everyone was stressed.

Ms. Wilkins, who was sitting beside me, made an announcement. In a board meeting that she had attended the night before, the superintendent asked, "What's the alternative to the alternative school?"

A callous school board member had responded, "Throw them in the street."

For Second Semester, Mr. Martin and Ms. Hackett's special education class had been split in two. Mr. Martin had a new paraprofessional named Ms. James, and Ms. Hackett was working with a new teacher named Mr. Osa. The new paraprofessional was a local woman, who used to be a bus driver, and the new teacher was a man who had emigrated from Nigeria.

"You should go talk to my new parapro," Mr. Martin told me, as he went to monitor the Time Out room. "She had a really bad day, yesterday."

The new special ed. parapro greeted me with smile. She was a petite woman in her fifties with blonde curls and a deep tan. She wore a track suit and sneakers, very sensible attire for working with alternative students, which readied her to spring into action. Ms. James was working as a paraprofessional, while studying to obtain her teaching certificate.

She was supervising three students while they did worksheets. She and Mr. Martin had only six students, so far, that semester, and three of them were absent. The smaller special education class was a breath of fresh air.

Actually, only two students did worksheets. The third teen was antsy. He laid on the floor, circled the room, fished through Ms. James's desk, and sat in a corner completely covered by his jacket. The paraprofessional spoke kindly to the kids calling them "Honey," "Sugar," and "Sweetie."

I couldn't ask Ms. James to elaborate on her bad day in front of the teenagers. "Yesterday was my first day alone with them, and it was hard," was all she could say. She wasn't totally new to the school. She did some substitute teaching at Peachtree Alternative, last year, and told me, "When I first saw that solitary confinement cell, I had to go outside and cry.

"As hard as it is, I know this is where I'm supposed to be," she said, impressing me, right away, with her dedication.

I stared at a big hole in the wall. Andrew had put it there, in a rage, earlier that morning. He punched it with a fist. Another boy saw me staring at the hole and said, "He was lucky he missed a pipe. He could have broken his hand."

An older special ed student wandered in, trailed by the hugging paraprofessional. "He's just checking things out," the woman explained and gave Ms. James one of her typical warm embraces. The boy showed us a hand wrapped in bandages. "What happened?" asked Ms. James. The boy had punched a wall, too, only he had punched a concrete wall and broken a finger.

"Why did you punch a wall?" I asked him.

"So I wouldn't punch a teacher."

Mr. Martin and Andrew come back from Time Out, and Mr. Martin shook his head at the students wandering around the room. "I should probably make you sit in your cubbies with your desks facing the wall," he told them. He turned to me and reported that Tom threw apples in the cafeteria, that morning, but I thought it was a tame disturbance compared to punching walls.

Mr. Martin and a boy teased each other. "Pick on somebody else, man," the boy told his teacher.

"You're the one who likes to argue," Mr. Martin said. "I like to argue, too." Well, that explained some of the odd exchanges I'd had with the man. He was a self-proclaimed contrarian. Understanding Mr. Martin helped me to warm up to him.

"Quinton's been lying on the floor, all morning," Ms. James told her partner. Quinton had also pounded on a computer keyboard and stood on a desk. Tom had spun around and around in Mr. Martin's chair and rolled back and forth across the room—all ADHD symptoms to my untrained eye.

"Sit down," Mr. Martin told a boy who was jumping around. He started to count to ten. On four, the boy perched on top of his desk; on eight, he lay fully across it, with his arms and legs dangling.

Someone threw a pencil. "Let me refresh your memory," the new parapro said. "If you throw something in this room, there's going to be a write up."

Special education was taking a field trip to the circus on Friday. Ms. Hackett urged me to come along, and the principal gave me permission. Extra chaperones were always welcome.

The lunchroom was thoroughly decorated for Valentine's Day. Betty had worked her magic, and the teachers' table had a red plastic tablecloth and a dish filled with candy hearts. That semester, though, most of the special education teachers ate lunch with the students. It was a new policy. The idea was that close adult proximity would deter student misbehavior. I asked Mr. Martin if the new policy worked.

"No, but it makes Ms. Henderson feel better," he said. "We have students with severe behavior problems," he added.

I ate with Mr. Osa, the new special education teacher, and learned more about him. He immigrated to America over twenty years ago. He attended a historically black college and earned a Ph.D. in agriculture. Mr. Osa made the transition to public school teaching for financial reasons, when he learned he could earn more as a teacher than as a college professor.

I followed him back to his room, Mr. Martin's old one, and noticed that Mr. Osa had added decorations. A round table was covered with a world map tablecloth. A globe sat on his desk and circus posters covered the walls.

The afternoon health lesson focused on stress. Ironically, a lot of stress resulted from the lesson, itself. "What is stress?" Mr. Osa asked the students, and two boys squabbled over who got to read the definition of stress from the textbook.

"I'm under stress," an ornery boy named Mark growled from a corner of the room. He was the boy who made me smile, one day, by making paper claws.

Ms. Hackett came into the room. "Why are you under stress?" she asked Mark.

"Because of you," he snapped.

"I'm sorry," said Ms. Hackett, refusing to get into a tussle.

"I'm tired and I have a headache," Mark whined. He charged across the room and grabbed Mr. Osa's textbook from his hands. The teacher didn't miss a beat and kept on talking.

Later, he took the book back and turned to thought questions at the end of the chapter. "What's the answer to question number one?" he asked the students.

"Don't know and don't care," Mark said, but Mr. Osa ignored him.

"What do you do to reduce stress?" the teacher asked a boy.

"Watch TV," the kid answered, and Mr. Osa told students that other ways of reducing stress were petting a dog, laughing with friends, or taking a walk.

"Answer the rest of the questions on paper," he told them.

"Heck, no," Mark said. "You answer them."

"Just do questions two through five," said Mr. Osa, with a tinge of frustration.

Mark's surliness was contagious. "How 'bout you do it?" another boy said to the teacher. The kid grabbed a pencil from Little Leon, who once brought a knife to school and threatened to cut off someone's finger. Leon retaliated, in a flash, by slamming a huge tin can in the vicinity of the thief's fingers. The can barely missed and thunked loudly on the table. It could have really hurt someone because Leon banged it with all his might.

"If you know what's good for you," Mark told the thief, "you'll give him back his pencil."

Leon started to have a tantrum. When Mr. Osa told him to sit down, he ran around the room, dodging the teacher. "Nah, nah, nah," he shrieked.

"Leon, you'll go to isolation," Mr. Osa warned, but Leon kicked a trash can and its contents spewed onto the carpet. He waved a piece of paper at Mr. Osa and yelled, "You're ill! You're ill!"

I then realized that Leon was echoing some anonymous adult who'd said those very words to him.

"He does this every day," Mark told me about Leon's tirade.

Mr. Osa got behind Leon and put him in a restraint hold by crossing his arms over the boy's chest. Leon's arms were pressed to his sides, and he kicked and screamed. "Go get someone," Mr. Osa told a custodian who had come into the room to empty the trash. She returned with the department chair.

The slender woman took over restraining Leon and wrestled him down the hall to Time Out. I followed and watched as Leon was put into the cell. Ms. Pearl was assigned to sit across from the cell and listen. Leon banged away and yelled, and the noise was blood curdling. The mostly unflappable Ms. Pearl looked distraught.

I asked if students were ever left in the cell unattended, and she told me that they weren't. She would rather physically restrain a student than put him inside a cell but she couldn't remember the technique. "I need retraining," she said.

Some of the boys on 200 Hall were enormous. "What if they're too big to restrain?" I asked Ms. Pearl.

"If they're too big, we get the security officer or they just walk out."

Leon banged on the door of his cell, and I winced at every blow. "Let me out! Let me out!" he screamed in a high-pitched voice.

Ms. Pearl told me that students were not supposed to have jackets, chairs, or shoelaces inside the cell. They were items that students might use to strangle themselves.

Leon banged away then threw coins up through the cell's mesh ceiling. He spit on the window. "Mr. Osa! Mr. Osa!" he yelled until Ms. Pearl lost her composure.

"He can yell 'til he's hoarse," she snapped.

There were other names for the solitary confinement cell at Peachtree Alternative School. Sometimes, students called it "the cave" and teachers referred to it as "the quiet room." Well, it was not quiet that afternoon.

When Leon finally settled down, Ms. Pearl told me to go ask Mr. Osa if he could come back to class. The teacher sent Ms. Hackett to retrieve the boy, who came back to the room, pointed at Mr. Osa, and yelled, "You're evil, evil, evil!" Again, I knew he was echoing words that some adult had used on him. Some adult had told Leon that he was evil.

"I told you to apologize," Ms. Hackett said to Leon. "Try, again."

"Sorry, Evil. Sorry, Evil," Leon said to Mr. Osa, and Ms. Hackett left it at that.

The new teacher wanted to explain to me what had occurred. He told me about chain reaction misbehavior and how it was important to stop it early. He blamed himself for not getting Leon's pencil back, immediately.

"I saw him slam that big tin can. He could have hurt someone," I said.

Mr. Osa started another lesson using math flash cards. He divided the class into two teams. The boys liked the competitive activity. They yelled out answers and solved some surprisingly complex math problems.

At 2:00 p.m., Ms. Henderson called a meeting of all paraprofessionals, in the library. The principal wouldn't be there but she had directed paraprofessionals to talk amongst themselves. A trash barrel and bucket were arranged, side by side, in the middle of the library to catch leaking rainwater. There were about a dozen paraprofessionals in the room—all women. Most of them were from the preschool, next door.

Ms. Hackett led the meeting. She reported that, the previous evening, the school board had made an announcement that affected paraprofessionals. "The superintendent recommended cutting ten paraprofessionals, county-wide," she told the group. "She also recommended cutting athletic programs in middle school and charging a fee for summer school." Ms. Hackett had heard the budget cuts would range from five to six million dollars in Peachtree County, alone.

The room was buzzing with concern. "We asked if those with seniority would be more likely to stay," said Ms. Hackett, "and the superintendent said she'd have to consult a lawyer."

"Remember there's going to be some natural attrition," Ms. Hackett tried to console the women. "The easy cuts are the retirements. P.E. teachers with no other certification areas may lose their jobs, unless they take the Praxis exam in other subjects. Golf and tennis will probably be cut, and the soccer team will have to rely on booster clubs for support." Naturally, they wouldn't cut football, I thought, feeling resentful on behalf of the golf and tennis players.

"They might possibly have night school instead of alternative school, next year.

"My personal opinion," said Ms. Hackett, "is that our jobs are pretty safe, here. For one thing, no one else wants to come here." The group tittered. "This is someplace you grow to love, and you're here because you want to be here. We even have gifted students.

"These kids aren't so bad. They're just kids who've made mistakes, and some have only made one mistake," Ms. Hackett said, and I was humbled by her compassion.

"When will we know about the cuts, for sure?" asked a woman.

Ms. Pearl joked, "Probably not until August, like last year. Probably, the day we come back."

Afterwards, as we were all leaving, Ms. Hackett told me, "They *have* to have paraprofessionals in special education. It's the law." She was reassuring herself about her own job.

Later in the day, I asked the special ed. department chair if she thought the alternative school was going to close. She didn't. Neither did the art teacher. "I plan on being here, next year," she said.

During gym, Mr. Osa tried to find out if a boy had been smoking. "Let me smell your fingers," he said. He sniffed but didn't smell smoke. Leon hurled a baseball bat into the depths of a dark closet, and one boy tried to kick another in the groin.

After school, the principal called a larger meeting in the library. Ms. Hackett stopped me, on the way in, looking flushed. "You know what I said, this afternoon, about things not looking so bad," she began. "Well, I may have been wrong."

On that ominous note, I joined the faculty in the library. "Just wait until you hear this," the counselor told us, taking a seat.

Ms. Henderson began the meeting. "I've been up and down over the future of this school. I've been to countless meetings. First, they weren't going to close the school, then they were, then they weren't. At yesterday's budget meeting, there was some erroneous information that this program costs $1.4 million to operate with only 85 students. Well, that was last year's figure . . . before we cut staff. This year, we've had 200 students come through the program, so far."

She told us about the board member, who suggested throwing alternative students in the streets, during a school board meeting. "I can't believe he said it in front of a packed house," Ms. Henderson said. "Ms. Wilkins and I had a long conversation, last night, about strategy, and we're going to put together a package of statistics. This board needs to know who we serve and what it costs."

Earlier in the day, the principal had received a phone call from the superintendent, who rarely called schools. The superintendent said they had a special board meeting and decided to close the alternative school.

"Teachers and cafeteria staff will be absorbed into other schools," Ms. Henderson said. "They're exploring other options for alternative students."

"What other options?" someone asked.

"Maybe night school from 3:00 to 7:00, like Stewart County. Students would drive themselves to school," said Ms. Henderson. She shook her head in disbelief and added, "They don't know our kids."

The art teacher had been sitting with her mouth open. "Do they really think," she began, "that our kids will drive themselves to school to complete their educations?" The other teachers made indignant noises.

"Apparently so," the principal said, in a tired voice. "Someone even suggested putting alternative students behind regular schools, in trailers surrounded by fences." That time, even I made a scoffing noise.

The principal shared another of the board's ideas, which was computer self-instruction. Alternative students would direct their own learning in computer terminals.

"They don't know our kids," Ms. Henderson said, again. "Students will be dropping out!"

She gave us a long, sad look. "I'm telling you this, now, because I didn't want you to hear it from someone else."

Teachers, who had been lulled into thinking the school would carry on, had been blindsided.

"I can't fight this any more," Ms. Henderson said. "It's not carved in stone but I'm telling you, right now, 'Go look for other positions.'" I watched Ms. Henderson's solemn face and thought that it had to be one of the low points of her career, having to disband a mostly stellar group of teachers.

She turned to the new assistant principal. "Do you have anything to add?" she asked him.

"Just that things can change on a dime," he said, which was no consolation.

The meeting ended, but a few teachers lingered.

"Throwing kids in the streets is what they'll be doing if they close this school," said Mr. Martin, recalling the board member's shocking words.

"Special education will be okay," Ms. Hackett reminded him. "By law, they have to provide it."

"They did this without consulting any experts!" Ms. Wilkins said about the board's decision. "They didn't ask any teachers. I am so mad!" She took a few deep breaths and tried to calm herself. "What you also need to know," she told the remaining teachers, "is that they may sell this property to a developer for millions of dollars."

The teachers were surprised because the school was located in a low-income neighborhood and was far from an interstate. "Who wants to develop *here?*" asked a teacher. "What's so appealing?"

"There's a pawn shop," the art teacher pointed out, facetiously.

"There's Peaches," Ms. W-J joked about a local prostitute.

"I'll tell you what," the counselor declared. "Why don't we send our worst students right back to regular school, first thing in the morning? That ought to teach them a lesson." She looked around for suggestions. "Who can we send?"

The teachers got into the spirit of retaliation and suggested several names. The jokes about revenge don't last long, though.

"They're safe here," the counselor said, mournfully. "At least they're safe at school. They get shot in the streets."

FEBRUARY 18

At the teachers' table, there was more bitter joking about sending the worst troublemakers back to regular schools. The art teacher mused about the concept of trailers surrounded by fences. "That would probably be an improvement over this place," she said.

Special education students came into the lunchroom, and Mr. Martin squatted beside my chair. "We had a hair burning incident," he reported. "Tom tried to impress a new girl with a lighter and it caught her hair on fire."

I spotted the girl in line and she looked okay. "It just singed her bangs," said Mr. Martin. "And Kenneth was trying to sell baby powder as cocaine."

The principal wasn't there, today, and teachers speculated that she was taking a personal day after yesterday's blow. "She needs to recover emotionally," someone said.

During breakfast, the school went into lockdown mode because a high schooler had threatened to bring a gun to school. Police officers arrived and were posted at the entrances, and students and teachers were sent to their classrooms.

The threatening note was just a prank, though, so students were allowed to change classes. Wanting to avoid the chaos of the gymnasium, I slipped into Ms. Cox's art class. She had a wide range of activities to choose from, and she gave directions quickly. Students could choose to do a scratch out, printmaking, or a mixed media project. Most kids chose scratch out, which required them to cover a poster board with crayon then apply black, soapy paint. After it dried, in a few days, they would scratch lines to create bold designs.

Ms. Cox didn't hesitate to do messy art projects, and alternative students rewarded her faith in them by being neat. No one splattered any paint.

The most challenging kid in the room wore some of his hair in a high ponytail on the side of his head. When he started dripping paint on the table, a girl cleaned it up for him and put newspaper underneath his work.

Another girl was researching Picasso on the internet. "Oh!" she exclaimed when she found one of his paintings, online. She called Ms. Cox over, and they both admired the image.

The kids did a good job of cleaning up, and even the troublemakers swiped their tables, a few times, with wet rags.

Ms. Cox answered her cell phone. "Yes," she told the caller, "detention is in my room. You have to be here at 3:15."

She hung up, grinning. "That kid was calling me from the gym," she told me. "Cell phones. You gotta love 'em."

FEBRUARY 20

I had low expectations for the circus field trip, given how exhausting the last field trip was. "If you're going to the circus, go to my room," the department chair told the students. "If you're not, go to Mr. Osa's or Ms. Singh's." I waited with the privileged kids and was actually glad to see that some of the most disruptive students were coming along. They probably needed a field trip more than anyone. Maybe a reward would help them. Some of them had never even been outside of Peachtree County.

We were a big group of twenty-three students and seven adults, including myself and the bus driver. There were eighteen boys and five girls. The department chair, Mr. Martin, Ms. Hackett, Ms. Pearl, and I were going along, as well as Ms. W-J and a handful of middle schoolers. I was the last person to leave the building, and the principal caught me by my elbow on the way out. "Watch him." She pointed to the biggest kid in line, a brand new boy named Gary. "He's a pedophile and he's eighteen and has been incarcerated. I didn't want him here." I was sure that she hadn't, considering there were 100 four year olds, next door, as well as middle schoolers and disabled students.

The principal was telling me to be her eyes and ears for the day. Gary was a pudgy young man with a buzz cut and a sprinkling of acne, who was wearing a gray track suit.

I wished I didn't know about him and didn't know that sex offenders rarely changed their ways. Now, I would be tense the entire trip. When I climbed on the bus, I positioned myself to keep an eye on Gary. Kim, the loud girl from Ms. Singh's class, had latched onto him. The poor girl was not discriminating. In fact, the last recipient of her affections had threatened to stab Ms. Singh in the forehead.

The students had to sit one per row, and Kim sat directly behind Gary. They sat sideways and shared Gary's headphones. He wore one earpiece, and Kim wore the other.

The department chair sat directly across from me. She tried to tease me by telling the other teachers, "Mary looks worried," and I couldn't deny it.

The circus was in an arena in the city. Before we left the school, the principal climbed on board to make an announcement. "They're expecting you," she said about the arena staff. "Remember that you're representing our school, and I expect you to be on your best behavior.

"Have fun," she added.

"Ms. Singh, do you know what 69 is?" Kim shouted.

The department chair put a stop to the sex talk by saying, "We're not going there."

On route, the boys in back entertained themselves by ogling girls, in the cars below, and they tried to get truck drivers to honk their horns. One trucker shot them a bird, and they howled with laughter.

The ride took almost ninety minutes. We exited the highway into downtown, and a boy behind me exclaimed about a homeless man sleeping under an overpass. As we neared the arena, we became stuck in traffic. Many other school buses were also headed to the circus, and several police officers were in the vicinity.

Behind me, a kid mused aloud about larceny. "If you snatched a purse around here, you'd get caught in no time."

"No, you wouldn't," said another boy. "You could hide in an alley."

"Leave anything you don't want searched," said Ms. Hackett. "I mean it! Don't take anything that will get you in trouble. No hats, no do-rags, no colors," she added, meaning gang colors.

The bus pulled alongside a curb, and I worried about students getting lost in the huge crowd. "Keep an eye on Jarrod," the department chair told Mr. Martin. "He might get lost."

She made Gary responsible for carrying the lunches into the arena, and he exited out the back of the bus with the cooler. We mixed with the throng and passed a mother and two children protesting animal cruelty by holding signs with the words "whips" and "chains" written in big red letters. As a former zookeeper at one of the best and most naturalistic zoos in the world, the Jersey Zoo in England, I had my own doubts about wild animal acts.

Ms. Hackett passed out tickets, and our group entered with no problems. We wound our way down a long flight of steps. A bank had donated our tickets so we headed for prestige seating. Bank staff in business suits ushered us through glass doors into a carpeted lobby.

The vendors with their nachos, glow sticks, balloons, and cotton candy were a big temptation, and alternative students immediately started asking me for money. We whisked them through the lobby, though, toward our excellent seats, just four and five rows up from the floor. I stopped worrying about losing kids when we were all seated.

The lights dimmed, and the show began. I hadn't been to the circus in almost thirty years and was impressed. It was a multicultural affair with a black master of ceremonies in a top hat and tailcoat. He introduced performers from around the world, including Brazilian trapeze artists and Chinese acrobats. The boys could hardly take their eyes off the pretty ladies in leotards. We learned that the circus had eighty animals and 250 support personnel. Elephants, camels, and horses paraded around the ring.

Mr. Martin had to stand in the aisle to keep the alternative students from running up and down the steps but I hardly noticed. We learned that elephants weighed approximately 9000 pounds and ate 250 pounds of food a day. A handful of alternative students were impressed, but most just looked bored.

Clowns threw pans of shaving cream, and I winced as a whip cracked and actually made contact with a horse's flank. Maybe the protesters were on to something. Chinese acrobats did flips, and the boys leaned forward as pretty ladies in glittering costumes walked on tightropes.

The house lights came up and it was time for intermission. I had to pass out lunches because I was the adult closest to the cooler. Even that task wasn't simple. Nothing was easy with alternative students. The kids wouldn't pass lunch bags down the row. They didn't seem to grasp the concept. "Just pass them," I insisted.

They were picky about their sandwiches. Some wanted ham and others, turkey, and I wondered why the lunches weren't exactly alike. We had similar disputes over plain and chocolate milk.

The other downside of being at the end of a row was I also had to collect the trash. It piled into my lap well before I finished my own sandwich but at least the kids weren't throwing trash on the floor.

I had forgotten about Gary who was sitting beside the department chair. She was keeping close tabs on him. Behind them was a long row of kinder-garteners, in private school uniforms, with battery-operated toys that lit up and spun around. When Gary needed to go to the restroom, the department chair escorted him.

"What's your favorite part?" I asked the boys beside me.

"That," said a boy, pointing to six motorcycles racing around inside a giant spherical cage.

Next, tigers were rolled out in cages, and some of the cats were enormous. That part of the show made me uneasy. I used to feed cheetahs, servals, and leopards at the Jersey Zoo, and I knew that wild animals were unpredictable. I told that to Mr. Martin who dismissed my fears and pointed to the tall chain-link fence encircling the ring of tigers. At the Jersey Zoo, I recalled, a serval had once escaped through a hole in the fence.

A man with a whip stood inside a circle of nine tigers and made them do tricks such as stand on their haunches and sit on stools. I was grateful that at least he didn't stick his head inside a tiger's mouth, as tamers did, historically.

Even though the ringmaster claimed there hadn't been an accident in over a hundred years, I didn't believe him. I supposed I was also wary from having watched too many dangerous animal episodes on TV. I didn't relax until the tiger act ended.

We decided to leave before the circus was over, and Ms. Hackett scooted us up the aisle. The kids were disappointed to leave early but it was a good idea. It would be too easy to lose them in a big crowd.

On the bus ride home, the department chair sat directly behind a boy and gave him a good head rubbing. She rubbed all around the top and sides of his do-rag, and he leaned back, smiling. "He really likes that," said Ms. Pearl.

I sat in the seat across from Gary, who eyeballed Kim's exposed shoul-der where her jacket had slipped off. Kim caught his eye and wiggled her shoulder.

Mark, the kid who made paper claws, was sitting in front of me. He insisted on keeping his window open. Ms. Hackett made him close it, but he opened it back up when she turned around. The wind was blowing on me, and I was freezing but I zipped up my jacket and suffered in silence.

At the moment, I was watching Gary, who slammed Mark's window shut. Mark slammed it open, swearing at the older boy, and didn't seem to realize that Gary was three times bigger than him.

Gary prodded Mark on the shoulder. "We'll take it outside, when we get back," he said. "You and me. Outside." He twisted his thumb in the direction of the window then sat down.

"Do you smoke?" Gary asked a middle schooler, in front of him, who had green eyes and long eyelashes.

"Sometimes," said the boy, and I leaned forward because the exchange smelled fishy. A few minutes later, Gary surprised the boy by handing him some cash. "What's this for?" the boy asked.

"Cigarettes," Gary told him.

The transaction worried me because sometimes pedophiles bought things for their victims in order to recoup the favor, later.

Kim had fallen asleep on her seat. As we neared the school, Gary shook her shoulder. "Wake up, sweetie," he crooned with mock familiarity. He shook her some more, and Kim pretended to keep on sleeping. He leaned in close. "Sweetie, wake up," he said, and I suppressed a shudder.

Ms. Hackett and I were the last ones off the bus. "What did you think?" she asked me.

"It went well."

"Aside from the fact they were running up and down the aisles, I think it did, too."

Chapter 8

March

MARCH 1

Mr. Owens was taking a few days off for a World War II reenactment in Florida. Not many public school principals would consider it an excusable absence but Ms. Henderson did. Peachtree Alternative School was so rough on teachers that they were allowed to take a few mental health days to pursue hobbies. I looked at Mr. Owens's elderly female sub and was glad it was her, not me, subbing.

I anticipated chaos in history class so I sought refuge in Ms. Bates's room. She was poised by a white board with a marker in hand. "Do I have a class today?" she asked me since her room was empty.

"It doesn't look that way."

Ms. Bates wrote the day's assignment on the board. "What about William?" she asked. "William is always here." She went into the hall in search of her students and managed to round up four of them: two girls and two boys. One girl wore a baggy gray sweatshirt and the other wore a sheer white shirt over a black bra.

The counselor walked in during morning announcements. "During the moment of silence," she told students, "I want you to think about set ups."

Later, she warned them not to encourage misbehavior in middle schoolers. High school boys, including our two, had egged a middle schooler into ogling the girl in the sheer shirt. The girl's name was Miranda.

"Andrew was just trying to impress you," the counselor told the boys. "He was showing off by walking funny down the hall behind Miranda." She thrust her pelvis forward and imitated Andrew's lewd walk. "Miranda doesn't need that. Do you understand?" she asked the boys, and they nodded.

Chapter 8

Figure 8.   Long Row of Boarded-up Windows.

Miranda wanted revenge. "I'm going to tell my mama," she said, threaten-ingly. "We know where he lives."

"Let's just leave it at that," said the counselor. "You can go to the front office to cool off, if you want."

"No, I need to call my mama," Miranda said, but the counselor didn't like her tone.

"I said you could go to the office," said Ms. Wilkins.

"You have to let me call my mama."

"Don't tell me what to do," said the counselor.

"I'll tell you whatever I want."

The counselor snapped. "Just go." She jabbed her finger at the door and shook her head as Miranda left. She told the rest of us, "I guess I made things worse."

The kids chose books for their thirty minutes of free reading, and the remaining girl chose a glossy young adult novel with a pair of thong under-wear on the cover. I was to blame for the risqué cover since I had donated stacks of young adult novels to the school, only a few of which I had actu-ally read. I received them free, in exchange for regular book reviewing for a parents' magazine. I could only hope the thong novel wasn't too racy.

One boy read *Z is for Zachariah,* a futuristic novel, and the other held a comic book and stared into space. "Is this all we're going to do? Just read?" he asked Ms. Bates, but she always had well-planned lessons.

Ms. Bates did sustained silent reading, too, and read a murder mystery at her desk. A timer on a shelf sounded every ten minutes to keep the kids from continually asking how much time was left.

Even though the lunchroom had no plastic knives, Ms. Bates wasn't worried about potential weapons lying around. She had a jar full of scissors on her desk.

Students began writing in their journals, and Ms. Henderson came in and whispered to Ms. Bates about résumés. Ms. Bates had missed the deadline to apply for a teaching position at another school. The two women talked about schools that were under construction in other counties, and I thought what a shame it was that Peachtree County would lose such talent.

The students' next assignment was to make singular nouns into plural ones. I tried it, myself, and struggled with the plurals of octopus and flesh.

Ms. Bates circulated and reassured students. "Sometimes, you just have to know the word," she said. "English is one of the hardest languages there is."

A boy finished his work and smacked his pencil down. "I'm fixin' to be seventeen," he announced and told us that he might go work for a pest control company, like one of his friends.

"My husband works for a pest control company," Ms. Bates said, then steered him back on task. "Where are you on your *Odyssey* project?" The boy hadn't even begun. He had to finish the book, create a map, and write a different ending. Ms. Bates never scrimped on activities, and the boy had plenty to keep him busy.

Miranda returned, and Ms. Bates gave her directions for the *Odyssey* project. "I'm not doing that," Miranda said.

"Why not?" asked Ms. Bates.

"Because I don't want to."

Ms. Bates's head shot back, balking at the girl's gall. "Oookaay," she said and walked away.

"I wish I could say that," the other girl told Miranda, "but I have to graduate."

Later, Ms. Bates slipped into a desk beside Miranda. "Bad day?" she asked.

"I don't understand this stuff," Miranda said, and they had a talk. Ms. Bates decided to rework some of her lesson plans, specifically for Miranda.

I hung around for second period, which was British Literature. The class was mostly white students, plus one black student and one Asian American. He was the only Asian student in the entire school, and I'd never heard him say a word. I certainly wouldn't categorize him as chronically disruptive so he had to be disaffected (withdrawn and apathetic).

One boy wore his hair in spikes, while another had long greasy hair that flopped in his face. The long-haired boy exuded great apathy. He moved slowly and wore layers of baggy clothing.

"Honey, do your journal for me," Ms. Bates told him.

"I'm tired," he said.

Ms. Bates took second period students on a snack run, and they returned loaded down with sugar. A girl sipped a sugary soda and ate from a jumbo bag of potato chips, even though it was only ten o'clock in the morning. She made plenty of noise by slurping, crunching, crushing the chip bag, and pounding on a computer keyboard.

"Wake up, babe," Ms. Bates told a boy whose feet were propped on the seat in front of him. The endearments came naturally to her and were actually welcomed by the at-risk teenagers. I suspected they didn't hear many endearments at home, and I was convinced they were a factor in Ms. Bates's successful classroom management. Not everyone could pull it off. Endearments probably also helped Ms. Bates think more kindly of students, when they were being frustrating.

A boy told Ms. Bates that he had a toothache but had to wait a month for a dentist appointment. *No one should have to suffer that long.* Ms. Bates urged him to speak to the part-time nurse to see if she could schedule an immediate appointment.

"You have a persuasive essay coming up," Ms. Bates told the class. "Write about something you feel strongly about but not the legalization of marijuana because I don't really care.

"Your essays can be school-specific. If you think we need a smoking area or lunch area outside, tell me that. They can be city-specific—something like Franklin needs its own newspaper—or state or country-specific."

The students filed to lunch. The cafeteria was half empty, and teachers didn't know why. Ms. Bates looked at the small crowd and marveled that it was so subdued. The high schoolers had sorted themselves into clumps of black and white students. One of the white boys wore a long black trench coat that disturbed me because it reminded me of ones worn by the shooters in the Columbine massacre.

Mr. Owens's substitute teacher joined us, and she looked authoritative in a turtleneck, glasses, and a tweed blazer. "How are they, today?" Ms. Bates asked the woman, and she just shook her head.

Ms. Bates spotted a boy with a super-caffeinated drink in his hand. "Oh, no. He's going to be bouncing off the walls."

"He's had two of them, already," the substitute said.

We watched the boy as he slugged his third caffeinated drink of the day and pretended to beat some drums on a lunch table. Ms. Bates teased him, "You should go to regular school so you can be in band." When the boy drummed even louder, Ms. Bates made him stop.

I decided to visit the substitute teacher, after all, and two girls in the class were being particularly sassy. They made fun of the substitute and talked back until someone warned them that I was a writer. "I'm sorry," one girl told me.

"I didn't mean it," said the other. *Too late, ladies. You should be apologizing to her, not me.*

Mr. Owens wanted his history students to take a test while he was gone. They settled down to work, although one girl passed her completed paper to a boy so he could copy from it. Kids had taken pencils from a jar and strewn most of them on the floor.

The kids turned in their tests, and the substitute teacher graded them using a key. "You're not concentrating," she said. "You're just putting down anything." The highest score in class was a 62.

I stared out the window and tried to ignore some boys, in the courtyard, who were making rude gestures at me. They appeared to be loose from special education. Outside a science class, there was a long row of boarded up windows.

As usual, there was a lot of noise coming from Mr. Wilson's math classroom. A big girl asked the sub if she can go to over there, and the woman let her.

It was a tame group compared to special education, but the students were equally unproductive. Some boys and Miranda, who wore another sheer top, pulled their desks in a tight cluster and started talking about a party. "I was getting high on weed," Miranda told them. While she was bragging about pot, another kid in the room was looking at marijuana websites on a computer.

The substitute teacher was sharp. "What are you looking at?" she demanded of the boy at the computer, who quickly shut it down. "Watch your mouths," she told some girls who'd been swearing.

The class was being defiant, but in subtle ways. A boy tossed a ball of paper at the trash can. He missed but didn't bother to pick it up. A girl did the same with an empty soda can but the substitute saw it land on the floor. "Whoever threw that can needs to pick it up," she said but no one moved.

"I am writing you up for talking," the substitute told a motormouth, who pretended to be scared.

The big girl wandered back from Mr. Wilson's room and hovered in the doorway. "Come back in," the substitute teacher told her.

"I'm not in this class, anymore," the girl said.

"Yes, you are."

"No, I'm not. I'm in Mr. Wilson's class." The girl wandered away.

We had only fifteen minutes left, and a girl asked to go brush her teeth. She was one of the few students at Peachtree Alternative whose parents could afford braces. She started gathering her things. "Leave your books," the substitute said. "It won't take you long to brush your teeth."

"You can kiss my ass," said the girl, grabbing her books and leaving.

The rudeness was typical but still jarring. The kids left and the substitute told me, "I'm glad I don't have to be here, every day." She thought that one of the problems was that Peachtree Alternative teachers were "too soft" on students.

That was the ongoing philosophical debate in a nutshell: lenient versus harsh alternative schooling. Who was more successful at reaching troubled teens: relaxed teachers or authoritarian ones? I was pretty sure I knew the answer but was waiting for the end of the year to issue my final verdict.

I wanted to photograph more of the building and began on The Derelict Hall. Just as I was loading my film, the principal rounded a corner and almost ran into me. "What are you doing?" she barked. "Where have you been?" I felt like a kid caught with my hand in a cookie jar.

Ms. Henderson was accustomed to using a forceful tone and wasn't disapproving, but she had broken my concentration. My creative juices had frozen so I put my camera away and called it a day.

MARCH 16

At another Save Our Students meeting, I asked Ms. Wilkins if the school board had discussed any more prospects for alternative students. "I don't know nothin' about nothin'," she said. "These children will be served," she paused for emphasis, "a little bit."

The Save Our Students director wanted to address the climate created by budget cuts and began the meeting with "matters of urgency." She shared some good feedback that Save Our Students received at a national at-risk youth conference. Other youth leaders praised her for the longevity of the organization, which had been in existence for a decade. It was the most collaborative county-wide organization for children in the state.

"Now, for the budget crisis," she said. The director reviewed programs that were heavily impacted by budget cuts. First, for discussion, was the elimination of Peachtree Alternative School. A gray-haired woman, wearing hot pink, told us that she was bewildered by the school board's plans to close the alternative school. "On behalf of Juvenile Court," she said, "Please help me understand what's going on. That's really why I'm here, today."

"The alternative school may be held, after hours, at Holly Springs High School," the director told her.

"Will they have a security officer?" the woman asked.

A deputy answered, "Yes, they will."

"There won't be any transportation, though," said the S.O.S. director. "It'll be up to parents to get alternative students to school." She frowned and said, "You can hardly get these kids to school on a bus."

Her frustration broke through, and she added, "If you could just see all these good teachers and the impact they have," she paused and tried to compose herself. "I am really grieving."

The juvenile court representative was still baffled. "If a district puts someone in alternative school for behavior reasons, how can it not provide transportation?"

"It's only required for special education students," someone else answered.

"Judges wrote letters to the Board of Education," the director said. "I don't know what else we can do. This property's going to be closed and put up for sale. It's twenty-three acres."

The next program impacted by budget cuts was S.O.S., itself. "Our offices have been in this building for ten years," said the S.O.S. director. "Right now, we're homeless."

Other sad news was that funding that supported family literacy was running out. The family literacy specialist told us about her endangered position but she didn't need to convince us of the importance of her work. "I promote literacy for families at home," she said. "I do a lot of collaborative work with the local technical college. We provide transportation and childcare so parents can access our program.

"We've placed thousands of books in homes and had family literacy nights and library events. I'm going to be looking for another job, soon. I love this work. I'm really going to miss it."

The tone of the meeting was solemn, and the bad news just kept on coming. Funding that supported transportation for an afterschool program in Great Oaks was also running out. "We have two hundred students who are getting tutoring," the program director told us. "Without transportation, we'll only have fifty or so. Transportation is critical, and it's very expensive."

"Amen," said a woman in back.

"This is what Save Our Students is all about," the director said, sweeping her arm across the room, "addressing these issues."

The health educator spoke, next. She was an articulate young woman who was a good advocate for children. Her face was flushed, and she spoke with passion. She pointed at the board, with its list of threatened and abolished programs and said, "Let's have a community forum to display the programs, and let citizens talk with officials. Maybe school board members will participate. We could have it in May." The group approved of the idea so the health educator would begin planning.

At least one person in the room was happy about the future. A county preschool coordinator was glad to hear that the mazelike preschool building, beside the alternative school, would be closed. "I'm excited that preschool is moving into regular schools. It makes a lot more sense to be in local schools, transportation-wise. I'm glad the board voted to move preschool."

MARCH 22

I learned I was pregnant, even though the fertility specialist had told me firmly that it couldn't happen. His exact words had been, "It would take a miracle." Well, a miracle happened.

My pregnancy made me warier about subbing at Peachtree Alternative School, where kids unduly stressed their teachers, not to mention went on rampages and threatened to stab people. I wanted to be extra careful during my first trimester.

I was supposed to substitute for Mr. Martin, who had taken to sounding anxious, himself, when he called me at home. Sometimes, he began his request for a sub by predicting there would be few students on the day he needed me. "We'll probably only have four or five students," he would say.

Mr. Martin was always grateful when I agreed to substitute, which slightly boosted my ego. Teachers at Peachtree Alternative knew their school was hardly a popular spot for substitute teaching, and they often told prospective subs, "It's an emergency."

In my days away from Peachtree Alternative School, I had managed to scare myself by reading a book called *Dangerous Fieldwork* by Raymond Lee. While the author did research in Northern Ireland, his advice could still be applied to observing in an alternative school. The author advised observers to carefully consider their dress, the location of their personal items, and their demeanor. I had been careful about all of those things. I hadn't drawn undue attention to myself by wearing tight clothing. I kept all of my belongings with me, at all times, and tried not to look like "a deer caught in headlights." I listened to my sixth sense and moved out of the way if I felt trouble brewing.

I arrived at the school to substitute for Mr. Martin, with three whole bookbags full of activities. Mr. Martin only left busywork, himself, so it was really best to bring my own materials. Jarrod hugged me, at breakfast, and I hugged him back. I had a special affinity for the boy. He ate his meals alone, near the teachers' table, and I sat with him, whenever I could.

The new policy of special education teachers eating with students had fallen by the wayside but I did it, anyway. I plopped down beside my charges, much to their dismay, and I was glad that Andrew, the trashcan thrower, was absent. I had a hard time forgetting the image of the heavy metal trash barrel bouncing off the department chair's back.

We had seven boys and a new girl named Vanessa, that morning. Vanessa wore a hooded pink sweatshirt, leopard-print pants, and spiked boots. She was quick to tell me that she wasn't supposed to be in special education. "I'm chronically disruptive," she said, embracing the label, "not learning disabled."

We walked to Cubby Room B, and Mr. Martin's new paraprofessional, Ms. James, was apologetic about the room's sterile appearance. "I hope it doesn't look bad to you," she whispered, gazing at the cubbies and the bare walls. "We've already gone through three substitute teachers, this semester. They won't come back."

I didn't plan on using the cubbies. Instead, I would work with small groups of students, in the middle of the room. Vanessa, of the leopard-print pants, had a terrible hacking cough. She told me that her father gave her forty dollars, over the weekend, to go buy cough syrup but she bought spiked boots, instead. Vanessa hacked some more, from deep in her chest.

"Sometimes a cough just has to run its course," I told Vanessa and planned to send her to the part-time nurse, as soon as she arrived. Ms. James handed me some language arts worksheets so I decided to give them a try. They were filled with obscure words that students would never use, and I started to stew about the work being totally irrelevant. The stack of worksheets that Mr. Martin had left was huge. When Vanessa wanted to write poems, instead, I heartily agreed.

The boys were growing restless. Legs were shaking, pencils were tapping, and one small boy was adding graffiti to the wall. He was a handsome kid with cornrows, Bermuda shorts, and a black down jacket. Ms. James moved him away from the wall and tried to encourage him to do some work. She passed Vanessa and patted her on the back. "Vanessa and I are going to do girly stuff on Friday. We're going to paint our fingernails," she said, and Vanessa grinned.

I decided to break out some of my own activities. They didn't align with curriculum standards but they might prevent chaos. "Mr. Martin told me you'd bring some stuff," Ms. James said, eyeing my bags.

We had a hard time setting up my animal slide show, from my days as a zookeeper. "You're going to see some animals you've never seen before," I said, wrestling with the equipment. In the meantime, one boy started rolling around the room in Mr. Martin's desk chair.

The kids liked the slides, and they particularly liked one of a large male orangutan. The ape's long arms almost touched the ground and his orange curls were several feet long. "He has dreadlocks!" a boy exclaimed.

The slide that interested alternative students the most was not one of animals. It was a slide of me aiming a tranquilizer gun, practicing for emergencies. They laughed at a picture of me shoveling manure, and I emphasized that zookeeping wasn't all glamorous. It involved plenty of grunt work.

Halfway through the show, it was time for lunch, so we left the equipment. The kids tried to take their lunch trays back to the classroom but Ms. James and I headed them off. I would much rather eat in the cafeteria, under the watchful eyes of Deputy Rodriguez and the principal, than have full responsibility for the students, myself. I needed a break. Somehow, though, Vanessa slipped past me and went to eat lunch in the department chair's room.

All of our boys sat in a line on one side of a table, and I sat across from them. "You can go sit with the teachers," a boy told me because I was spoiling his fun. I told him I was happy where I was.

Things were quiet during lunch. The handsome boy in Bermuda shorts and a down jacket decorated his hamburger with kernels of corn then paid for a second burger. Betty, the cafeteria manager, came over and slipped another boy a treat, a container filled with grapes from the salad bar.

Back in the classroom, we looked at kangaroos, and I told kids how to catch them. You grabbed them by their tails and held them away from your body so their powerful hind legs wouldn't kick you and their toenails wouldn't scratch.

To fill more time, I passed out a handout filled with animal skeletons. "What animals are these?" I asked the kids, and they had no trouble identifying giraffe, alligator, elephant, frog, and kangaroo. We also looked up various animal habitats on a world map. Later, I quizzed students and gave them animal stickers, as rewards.

Next, we headed outside to play with an old parachute that I'd bought at an army surplus store. Several boys volunteered to help me retrieve it from my car. It was funny that even chronically disruptive students enjoyed doing favors for teachers, especially if it involved leaving the building.

On the field behind the school, Vanessa's spiked heels stuck in the grass, and kids began to fan out. To reel them back in, I unfurled the parachute. The big green circle was twenty-four feet in diameter. It billowed in the wind and served as a kid magnet.

We all grabbed hold. First, we made ripples then we made waves. We raised the chute high above our heads then lowered it to our ankles. It was a big piece of material, and all of the kids were smiling. We made a mushroom by raising the parachute high then ducking inside and pulling the edges beneath us. We sat inside the dome and looked at each other in the green light.

Everyone grinned, and I relished the happy moment. Vanessa sat with her spiked heels splayed in front of her, and Ms. James warned her not to puncture the fabric. Our dome sank, slowly, until we were covered in nylon.

Back in the sunshine, we divided into teams and tried to bounce a pink ball off the other team's half of the parachute. My team scored point after point. Waving the chute in earnest, though, was exhausting, and all the kids collapsed on the grass. We did one more mushroom before rolling the parachute up for good. Only then, did I notice the many pieces of broken glass in the grass and hoped that no one had been cut.

For our next activity, Vanessa and I set up a launch pad using a big bucket that we turned upside down. On it, we placed empty film canisters. I poured a small amount of water into each canister then dropped in Alka-Seltzer tablets. At my signal, the kids quickly snapped on lids and stood back. The lids blew high into the air with magnificent pops, delighting the students.

"It's hard to believe something so simple can be so entertaining," said Ms. James, and I thought that setting off explosions probably wasn't the most appropriate thing to be doing with aggressive chronic disrupters. Still, it was a classic science activity that students enjoyed.

I tried to add some variety. "What happens if we shake one of the containers?" I asked. It exploded even faster. "What happens if we set it on the launch pad upside down?" The container, not the lid, went flying into the air. I followed the activities with a discussion of chemical reactions.

"Are you going to be our teacher, tomorrow?" a boy asked.

"No, Honey, but maybe later," I told him. I found myself using a lot of endearments, like Ms. Bates. I checked my watch to see how much time had passed. Not nearly enough.

Running through all of one's activities, early in the day, could happen at any school. That was why overplanning was so critical. I had just a few things left in my bags.

Back in Cubby Room B, I pulled out felt-tip markers and some designs for the kids to color while I read aloud. I read Christopher Paul Curtis's book *The Watson's Go to Birmingham—1963*. I'd actually gotten to meet Mr. Curtis on a safari in Kenya, and he was as humorous as his book characters.

"We're not listening," a boy told me but I'd heard that before and was able to respond calmly.

"That's okay," I said. "I like reading aloud, even to myself."

The kids squabbled over markers and talked amongst themselves but I forged ahead, believing that reading aloud to kids was invaluable. If I were Mr. Martin, I would do it on a regular basis.

"Are they black?" a boy asked me, about the book's main characters.

"Yes," I said. The brothers in the book teased each other, squabbled, and got into jams, and my students chuckled just often enough that I knew they were listening. The kids showed me their bold designs, and I made admiring comments. Ms. James further validated their artwork by taping it to the windows, and I thought that having a collegial paraprofessional was a really great thing.

Before gym, Vanessa told me, "Thank you for bringing the parachute." Ms. James had told her to say it but I was still touched, and I praised her for being so polite. Manners were not usually a strong suit of Peachtree Alternative students.

Half of our kids headed to gym and half went back outside. "Where should I go?" I asked Ms. James.

"Wherever you want. You've worked hard, today," she told me. I chose the gym and sat on the bleachers beside Mr. Osa, Ms. Singh, and Ms. W-J from the middle school.

"How did it go today?" Mr. Osa asked me.

"Pretty well," I said.

He asked Ms. W-J where she would be, next year, and touched a nerve. "In court, probably," Ms. W-J answered, flatly. She was in a double-bind because not only was the alternative school closing, but P.E. programs were being cut and her certification area was physical education. "I'm one of those expendable P.E. teachers," she said. "I think they're just punishing me for having been here ten years. I have more seniority than most people, here, but the county's offering them contracts instead of me."

Mr. Osa didn't help matters by asking, "Can't you just take an exam in another field?" Ms. W-J responded that the exams weren't cheap and went back to grading papers.

Across the gym, Little Leon from Mr. Osa's class was clambering on some broken gym equipment. He swung on some listing parallel bars then straddled a vault. A couple of boys joined him, and I could have sworn that I saw Leon flick a cigarette lighter.

The boys were definitely up to something. They shot me glances, which I recognized as furtive teacher checks, and one of them scooted in front of Leon to shield him from my view. I enlisted Ms. Singh, and she headed over in an intentionally languid manner. It reminded me of the way I approached my dog when I was trying to catch her by the collar, moving slowly but with stealth. Ms. Singh was a petite woman but she didn't look like a pushover in her black leather jacket. She made the boys turn their pockets inside out but found nothing. They shot me dirty looks from across the gym, and I was embarrassed to have sent Ms. Singh on a wild goose chase.

Afterwards, the boys headed over to complain. "Did you say I had a lighter?" Leon asked me.

"Yes. Did you?"

"No!" he growled and stomped away.

At the bus stop, the special education students wrestled, exactly what they were not supposed to be doing in the vicinity of big vehicles. The department chair passed out some graded papers but many of them ended up as crumpled balls on the asphalt. A big boy from her class made fun of an effeminate boy by flopping his wrists and swishing his behind. I saw a flash of pain in the victim's eyes but didn't act quickly enough to stop the bullying, and the kids boarded the buses.

I thought about the incident for a long time, afterwards. Protecting students was a primary responsibility of teachers. Students had to feel safe at school, and I'd failed in the schoolyard. I could only resolve to do better.

MARCH 23

Save Our Students had called a special strategizing meeting on behalf of the school, and a dozen people gathered around a long table in the meeting room. A blonde parole officer swept aside some papers to make a spot for me.

She was upset about the night school concept. "Please forgive me but this is the most ridiculous thing I've ever heard! They've got to be joking!" she said about the school board. "If we sweep kids under the carpet, they are *not* going to go away."

Beside her, the brunette parole officer predicted, "Gangs are going to increase. Teen pregnancy will increase." The night school concept was sounding crazier by the minute.

The health educator added, "You'll definitely see more risky behaviors in terms of sex and drugs. Kids will be bored. They'll have no supervision. Parents have to work. They can't quit their jobs. People who aren't sitting in this room will have their homes broken into."

A boys and girls' club director jumped in. "Down the road, this county will pay so much more, whether it's for bigger jails or more health care. This is not saving money! It costs four times as much to educate them in prison!"

"It bothers me very much," said the blonde parole officer, "that the school board has no idea what goes on in here. Teachers reach the most unreachable kids, and no one has been as beneficial as that woman over there." She pointed to Ms. Henderson, and we give the principal a round of applause.

The brunette parole officer told us that Peachtree Alternative was the best alternative school she visited because teachers really knew the students.

The principal repeated a prediction that she had made, earlier in the year. "I give whatever program they put in place, six months, but my people will be gone. They're probably going to hire new young teachers, who'll do it for the money, but they won't last two weeks."

"These kids are being set up to fail," said the blonde parole officer. "They're not going to attend night school, and they're going to offend prior to three o'clock."

A sheriff added, "I told my men, 'You guys better get ready because if they go through with this, the 911 calls are going to go through the roof.'" It was an ominous prediction from a law enforcement officer.

"I think we might be overreacting," said a social worker, and her partner agreed.

"This is not tiddlywinks we're talking about," the sheriff told her. "These kids are hardened. They need structure." The parole officers nodded.

The group discussed the other option under consideration for alternative students—computer self-instruction. A man, sitting to my right, was taking so many notes that I wondered if he wasn't a reporter. He told us that he used to teach at an alternative school in another county. "If students could handle that," he said of computer self-instruction, "they wouldn't be here. If you ever use the term self-paced with at-risk kids, then you're dead in the water. They'll use the excuse, 'I'm working at my own pace'." I didn't think he was being too cynical and happened to agree that computer self-instruction would be futile for the majority of alternative students.

A deputy suggested a program called PROMISE for violent offenders. Teens had physical activity, such as sit-ups, in the early mornings then showered and ate. They were escorted to school, and their officers were readily available for consultations. After school, teens went to tutoring then counseling, along with their parents.

"We talked about PROMISE once," said Ms. Henderson. "We could have worked it into our program."

"Why didn't you?" someone asked but the deputy answered for her.

"The school board had some concerns about the boot-camp style, in-your-face sort of things," he said, and a parole officer scoffed.

Ms. Henderson tapped her heart and said, "To work with these kids, you have to have something in here."

The S.O.S. director tried to come up with another solution. "Maybe a judge could meet with the school board," she said, thinking it might give them a better understanding of the consequences of closing the alternative school.

Ms. Henderson doubted that the school board would be interested in such a meeting. "They've never even walked in the door to see what we put up with on a daily basis. No one has ever asked our opinion on any of these changes."

"Not asking Ms. Henderson or Ms. Wilkins about their opinions was a real slap in the face," said the blonde parole officer.

"The people who are making the decisions don't know what we do," said the principal. "I don't want to keep this old building open but I don't want to see kids on the streets."

A deputy wondered aloud if any board members had kids in the public schools, and a woman answered that a couple of them had grandkids in the schools. "Their kids are going to be affected by this population," the deputy said.

The S.O.S. director tried to steer the meeting towards resolution. "This group needs to come up with a suggestion that is mutually acceptable," she said.

"Scare people," the deputy said. "Tell them the consequences. Tell them what happens when kids hit the streets."

"No, don't," said someone else. "That'll just make things worse. We've got to downplay the danger."

Some people in the room, such as deputies and parole officers, perceived alternative students to be dangerous and barely redeemable while others, such as counselors and social workers, perceived them as more benign and salvageable. If we couldn't define the problem students, how could we propose a solution? And if people in the trenches were struggling for answers, you could almost understand the school board's confusion.

"Can we have an alternative school in a church?" a woman asked but others told her that would violate the separation of church and state.

"If we serve alternative students between 12:00 and 4:00 rather than 4:00 to 8:00," said Ms. Henderson, "we wouldn't have to feed them and it would save money. Meals cost a lot.

"Holly Springs parents will get their kids to alternative school, whatever the hours," the principal said. "It's the Franklin group that won't come."

"I'm coming up cold as far as solutions go," the S.O.S. director said. "Other counties are expanding their alternative programs. The most logical thing, to me, is to keep Peachtree Alternative School open. It works, which is why it's so hard to come up with other ideas."

A lot of important people were passionately against the dissolution of Peachtree Alternative School.

The principal just sounded resolved. "I'm laying low," she told us.

The S.O.S. director wrapped up the meeting. "This is sadder than sad to me," she said about the looming closure.

MARCH 30

Mr. Osa had called in sick, that morning, and I was asked to substitute at the last minute. Even though I didn't have my substitute teaching kit with me and had an aversion to "winging it," I agreed. Mr. Osa's room was dark so I flicked on the lights and was surprised to find a boy squatting under a table. "How are you, Mark?" I asked but he didn't answer. I asked, again, and got no response so I gave up. Two more kids came in and were thrilled to learn that I was substituting for Mr. Osa. One small boy actually jumped up and down with glee. Their joy, I suspected, was due to their anticipation of an easy day with a substitute.

"She's nice," a boy said about me, although I was sure he was trying to butter me up. "Can we watch a movie?" he asked in the next breath.

"We'll see," I said. There were only four boys, total, and surely I could handle four boys, even if two of them were ornery Mark and Little Leon. Ms. Hackett, my experienced paraprofessional, began to run the show and I gratefully surrendered my authority . . . just like Mr. Martin.

Ms. Hackett prepared to lead a discussion on *The Watsons go to Birmingham—1963.* The boys had read the entire book and were surprised to learn that I had, too. I told them that the author, Christopher Paul Curtis, was a big man with dreadlocks, or at least he had dreadlocks several years ago. I had met him on a trip to Kenya for the nonprofit foundation Children's Literature for Children, which helped build school libraries in developing countries. "He likes to tease," I told the boys, "just like his characters tease in his books. Christopher teased me in Africa by saying, 'Why don't you go tickle that giraffe's knee?' or 'Why don't you pull on that baboon's ear? That would have earned me a good kick or bite." Some inspiration that I was able to share was that Christopher struggled for years, as a writer, before making a breakthrough with *The Watsons Go to Birmingham,* which was a Newbery Honor. He even wrote during his breaks, while working on an assembly line in a Detroit auto factory. "Now, that's persistence," I told them.

I joined three boys at a table in front of Ms. Hackett's desk, and the only boy who didn't come over was Mark, who preferred to sulk in a corner. He threw a few sullen quips our way but warmed up when the discussion became lively. Later, Ms. Hackett revealed that Mark really should have been placed in a psychoeducational program because his behavior problems were so severe.

The boys at the table had a great discussion about the book. They talked about sibling rivalry and scary moments such as when the main character, Kenny, almost drowned. Mark interrupted us by displaying a picture that he had drawn of his grandmother as a troll.

The climax of the historical fiction book was the bombing of the Sixteenth Street Baptist Church. Ms. Hackett distributed a poem about the bombing, "Ballad of Birmingham" by Dudley Randall. The kids had already read it several times. They had discussed the Civil Rights Movement and even watched historical footage from the 1960s. Ms. Hackett handed me a copy of the poem. "Miss Mary, why don't you read it," she said. "You might have a different inflection in your voice."

I read the poem, as clearly as possible, and tried not to cry. It was a powerful piece about the violence against protesters in Birmingham, Alabama, and a mother's decision to send her child to church rather than participate in a march. It was the wrong decision, and the daughter died in the Sixteenth Street Baptist Church bombing. One boy knew the poem by heart and recited the words as I read them aloud.

"Wow," I said, when I finished the poem.

"As a mother," said Ms. Hackett, with her hand on her heart, "that gets me every time. It gives me chills." She raised her sleeve to reveal goose bumps on her forearm, and I revealed mine. The boys looked for goose bumps on their own arms.

Leon went over and sat inside a brown cardboard box in the corner. He covered his head with newspaper. He was hiding, just like a toddler. When Ms. Hackett asked him a few questions about the Civil Rights Movement, he answered from beneath newspapers and his voice was muffled.

I told the boys about the Birmingham Civil Rights Institute, where I used to volunteer. It was directly across the street from the Sixteenth Street Baptist Church. "I wondered, sometimes, if the museum wasn't too scary for children," I said, "because it had statues of leaping, snarling German Shepherds and a real bombed out bus, damaged during the Freedom Rides." The boys all told me that they wouldn't be scared in the museum.

I couldn't let Ms. Hackett do *all* of the work so I borrowed a couple of math games from across the hall. When Ms. Hackett stepped out of the room, Mark and Leon started wrestling wildly, and nothing I said would stop them.

"Come help me pick out a math game," I suggested, to no avail. I tried to refrain from shouting. The boys kept on wrestling, and books and papers were knocked off tables. In my pregnant state, I was not going to touch them and they finally stopped on their own.

I proposed using math flash cards but that idea was shot down by a panting Mark. Instead, the boys chose math tic-tac-toe. I put Mark and Leon on separate teams, and the five of us gathered around a table in the middle of the room. Time flew as the boys did math problems and placed their tiles.

A boy's stepfather came to visit. Parent involvement was rare at the school, and Ms. Hackett thanked the man profusely for coming. He watched us struggle with math problems, said a few stern words to his stepson, then left. Later, Ms. Hackett told me that the boy's behavior had improved dramatically since his mother had remarried.

At lunch, Ms. Hackett and I ate with the kids. The principal did paperwork at a nearby table and fussed at the boys for being too loud, even though they were hardly making any noise at all. I thought that everyone had their bad days.

A boy asked a question about an absent classmate, who had threatened to commit suicide. Ms. Hackett hushed him by saying, "I'm not going to talk about it. If you want to speak to a counselor, tell your parole officer but we're not going to talk about it, here."

After lunch, we studied volcanoes in a science textbook and drew volcano pictures. Mark was a good artist and drew volcanoes spewing rocks, plumes of smoke, and rivers of molten lava. It was one of my more productive days in special education, thanks to Ms. Hackett.

Chapter 9

April

APRIL 1

Ms. James called me, late at night, and asked me to substitute in Mr. Martin's room. Her uncle was very ill in the hospital. *How could I say "no" to such a lovely lady, under the circumstances?*

Mr. Martin told me, at breakfast, that things had been rough, lately. Andrew, the trashcan thrower, had been acting up. "He's off his medication," Mr. Martin said. One student had already been sent home for shoving a teacher.

Ms. Pearl came in to borrow our telephone and called another boy's father. "You have to pick him up," she told the man. "He's out of control." *It was only eight in the morning and, already, we'd lost two students from special education.*

During breakfast, Ms. Hackett asked me, "Would you like to substitute tomorrow?"

"No. It's too hard, and I'm pregnant," I blurted out to the entire table. I knew I was being wimpy but I was worried. I'd had two previous miscarriages and wanted to do everything possible to protect my third pregnancy, including minimizing stress.

The special education teachers congratulated me. "I thought you were adopting," said Ms. Pearl.

"We still are," I told them. "Now, we'll have two children."

"What a blessing," said Ms. Pearl.

Mr. Osa stopped me in the hall and put in his two cents about subbing. He practically begged me to substitute for him and Ms. Hackett, the following day. He would be gone in the morning, and Ms. Hackett would be gone in

Figure 9.   Damaged Ceiling Tiles.

the afternoon. Mr. Osa assured me that I wouldn't be in the classroom alone. I caved in and agreed to substitute.

I headed on to Ms. James's room, where Mr. Martin apologized for not having any lessons planned and asked me to copy some worksheets from a stack of workbooks. In his defense, he had been in charge of Time Out that week. I copied the assigned pages, plus some origami directions from my substitute teaching kit. I also had word searches, mazes, markers, and several middle-reader novels, in case the worksheets didn't cut it.

Mr. Martin helped me out by sending a couple of boys to the department chair's room and taking some disruptive students with him to Time Out. I was left in the room with only Andrew, Tom, and Vanessa who wore spiked boots. Tom started in on worksheets, and Vanessa whined for help. Andrew occupied himself by trying to reattach a broken pencil sharpener to the wall.

As the only girl in class, Vanessa had my sympathy, and I let her be demanding. "Come help me with this," she said, and I leaned over her paper. She still had a dreadful cough but at least she had seen a doctor. Sometimes, she forgot to cover her mouth, and I felt the droplets spray me.

At my suggestion, we did origami, and Vanessa liked it so much that we made an endless variety of shapes. I had an assortment of colored paper for her to choose from. I grew weary but kept on folding. We made rabbits, birds, flowers, frogs, picture frames, and secret letters, and Vanessa took them all across the hall to show the department chair. I thought Vanessa probably had a crush on the woman, and sometimes the department chair would even let Vanessa braid her hair.

"Fight! Fight!" someone shouted in the hall, and I struggled to keep my three charges inside the room. They pressed their faces against the small square window in the door, as Deputy Rodriguez ran past.

Graffiti was sprouting in Cubby Room B, and one wall had a gaping hole in it where Andrew had punched it. He had taken to subtly dropping candy wrappers and empty soda cans into the hole where they would probably draw mice, rats, or roaches.

Mr. Martin wanted us to bring our lunches back to the classroom. I tried to eat all my food in order to be a role model for proper eating. My institutional hamburger, though, had wads of gristle and I spit them out.

Tom was my lone charge in the afternoon, and we sat in the cubby room with the lights off. He worked diligently by himself, for awhile, then we played some math games.

Mr. Martin dropped off his crew from Time Out and disappeared. It was almost time to go outside but first we had to clean up the room. One boy leaned over and tried to tell me a dirty joke but I cut him off. Several boys wandered into the hall, and I couldn't get them to come back in. It was funny how they acted as if you were invisible. When Ms. Wilkins started down the hall, though, they scrambled back into the room.

Mr. Martin returned and spotted some tater tots on the floor. "Go get a broom and dustpan from the lunchroom," he told a boy, and I accompanied him. The boy stopped abruptly outside the cafeteria, which was filled with preschoolers. "I can't go near the Pre-K," he told me. "They think I'll hurt them but I won't."

Who thought that? Parole officers?

"My cousin is in Pre-K," the boy said. "and I wouldn't hurt him." I wondered what on earth the twelve year old had done that made him a danger to small children. "I'll go wait in the office," the boy told me, as he backed away from the cafeteria. He removed himself from the vicinity, while I fetched the broom and dustpan, myself.

The boy carried the items back to the room and practically hugged the wall to avoid being near four year olds who were heading to the building, next door. I watched the backs of preschoolers' heads with their beads and curls and bows and thought how small and vulnerable they were.

The episode made me terribly, terribly sad. What was the world coming to when children were endangered by other children?

Mr. Martin warned me to make sure that students didn't smoke during free time. Outside, during the break, the boys sat on a jungle gym and Vanessa sat in a swing. "Do you want company or do you want to be by yourself?" I asked Vanessa, since you never knew with teenagers.

"Company," she said so I sat in a nearby swing that was too small and squashed me. Vanessa wanted to talk. She had considered running away, over the weekend, because she was tired of adults yelling at her all the time. She had called her parole officer, instead, who encouraged her to stay home. Vanessa's parole officer was Alice, the pretty brunette. Vanessa was proud that Alice didn't put an electronic anklet on her. "Alice trusts me," she said. Alice had also given her a book on "girl power" that was back in the classroom.

The restless boys wanted to go to the gymnasium. The group hurried away, and I scurried after them. No observer would have ever guessed that I was the one in charge. Ms. Wilkins spotted the passel of kids and thought they were alone, at first, because I was so far behind them.

Outside the gym, Tom rode a bicycle that he claimed was his own. He steered it through the doors of the gym and onto the basketball court, where Ms. Pearl took it away. The bathrooms smelled so bad, that afternoon, that most people hunkered on the far side of the gym. Some boys scrimmaged and Vanessa, Ms. Pearl, and I sat high in the bleachers.

Vanessa tortured us by reading aloud her entire "girl power" book but we endured it for the sake of education. It was good for her to read aloud. We all learned that when we were in a bad mood, we were supposed to take a bubble bath, put on silky pajamas, and paint our fingernails.

I watched boys scrimmage, and it nearly killed me when thirsty kids forgot that the water fountains didn't work. We, adults, really should have made a big stink about the broken fountains and brought water with us to the gymnasium. The lack of water bordered on being a human rights violation.

Vanessa droned on for an hour, until she finished the book. "That's great, Vanessa. You're a good reader," I told her when she finished, thinking that every book an at-risk kid read was a victory.

APRIL 12

Mr. Martin had jury duty so I agreed to fill in. As I headed down 200 Hall, I learned that his parapro, Ms. James, was out, too. She had sprained her ankle by jumping rope with teenagers in Sunday school. I felt sorry for her but it was bad, bad news for me. It meant I would be alone with Special Education Severely Disruptive (SESD) middle schoolers.

Andrew, Tom, and four other boys were already in the room. The biggest boy was the silent type, a rarity in 200 Hall. I told the students that the new school superintendent was visiting, later, so they should be on their best behavior but it meant nothing to them.

As we headed to breakfast, students from Mr. Osa's class spotted me and jumped up and down. "Are you going to be our teacher?" a boy asked eagerly, and I couldn't help but smile at his display of enthusiasm.

"No, I'm subbing for Mr. Martin, today."

Ms. James had called in a substitute paraprofessional to help me but I would have rather been alone. The substitute had no energy. I had seen her, several months ago, sleeping in the bleachers when she should have been watching kids on the gym floor. I shuddered to think how the students would act today with two substitute teachers. The other sub was working towards a teaching certificate in special education, which I found hard to believe, given her lethargy.

Over at the cash register, Betty sang a good morning tune. "It's a beautiful morning," she sang, and some teachers smiled at her cheer. It was a good show for the new superintendent, who was visiting and stood in the doorway.

"Who are you, today?" Ms. Hackett asked me.

"Mr. Martin and she's Ms. James," I said, pointing at the substitute paraprofessional. Ms. Hackett did a double-take as the bad news registered. She knew that trouble was in store.

My students ate French toast sticks at the far end of the lunchroom. "I should be able to handle six boys," I told Ms. Hackett, without much confidence.

Back in our room, I tried to get started. No assignments had been left for us, even though Mr. Martin had known about jury duty, for several weeks. There was no schedule of activities printed on the board. What was I supposed to do? I floundered, looking through stacks of books for ideas but I didn't flounder very long. If I showed uncertainty, the boys would take advantage of me.

As I was ruffling through my substitute teaching kid, the responsible Ms. James phoned from her bed and spoke to the substitute paraprofessional. Afterwards, the woman produced some worksheets from Ms. James's desk. Only Tom and Andrew would do them. I played math games with a couple of other boys.

The room was actually pretty quiet. I couldn't believe that Andrew was concentrating so hard on his worksheets, and I had fun playing math games. Even the volume of the television was low. Normally, students tried to blast it. Ms. Henderson and the new superintendent chose that moment to look in, which was my good luck.

Tom and Andrew had completed all six of their worksheets, and I took the time to check them. Tom's work was a mess. He had just filled in random answers. I tried to go over it, anyway. Ms. Pearl had told me that Tom was better behaved, last year, and I wondered what had changed in his life.

Andrew's answers, on the other hand, were mostly correct. "Good job, fellow," I told him.

From Ms. James, we had learned that the boys were supposed to read *The Pearl*. I pulled seven copies off a shelf, distributed them, and began reading aloud. A boy mimicked me, as I read, which really didn't bother me. Echoing important words was fine. "Do you want to read aloud?" I asked the boy, and he gave it a shot.

Lunchtime rolled around. "Can we eat in the room?" a boy asked but I was tired of being in charge. Let the deputy keep an eye on them in the cafeteria. "No."

"Aww, come on," the boy whined. "Let's eat in the room." I stood firm but he wrote on the board, anyway, "Attention, we are eating in the room, today."

"No, we're not," I announced but didn't bother to erase his words.

"I'm going to eat in Ms. Singh's room," Tom told me.

"No, you're not."

We headed for the cafeteria, and I stood guard by the door to keep the boys from escaping with their trays. They veered away, towards a table, except for Tom who ducked past me. "Tom, you have to eat in the cafeteria," I told him.

"No, I don't."

The substitute parapro backed me up. "Yes, you do," she said. Tom tried to hide from us by slipping into the smelly boys' bathroom with his lunch tray. I was surprised by the length to which he would go to avoid following directions. "I can't believe he's eating in the bathroom," I said to no one in particular.

"Yuck," said a teacher, who was passing in the hall.

Tom left his tray in the bathroom but brought his hamburger into the hall. He stuffed his face, and the situation was just too funny, to me. I remembered "Do not engage in power struggles" was of the cardinal rules of teaching chronically disruptive students. I really didn't care where Tom ate his lunch so I headed back to the cafeteria, and Tom took his tray to Ms. Singh's room.

I collected my lunch and sat beside Mr. Osa. He told me that Mr. Martin was unlikely to be chosen for jury duty because lawyers didn't like to take teachers away from schools. I sincerely hoped he was right. If Mr. Martin and Ms. James were gone all week, I was really in trouble.

I asked Ms. Hackett for some classroom management suggestions. "Are they in their cubbies? Keep them in their cubbies," she told me but I couldn't bring myself to do that. I taught best when I could move freely amongst students, squat beside them, and do hands-on activities.

Back in the classroom, Andrew told me, "I ain't doing no more work," before settling down to a geography activity from one of my game books.

I did the activity, too. (My education hero, Martin Haberman, was a firm believer in working alongside students, whenever possible.) Andrew was a smart kid, and he whizzed through his work.

The hugging paraprofessional replaced the substitute paraprofessional, temporarily, so she could go to the bank. I wondered aloud why the substitute was going to the bank in the middle of the day. "I hope she comes back," the hugging parapro said about the sub. "One time, she didn't." We watched the kids work, and she told me, "They behave better for you than they do for Mr. Martin."

I thought, again, that it probably had to do with elbow grease. Mr. Martin didn't apply it.

I checked geography papers and made students redo their wrong answers. Half of the class had participated in the activity while one boy slept, one drew pictures, and Tom wandered around the room. Sadly, a fifty percent participation rate was a roaring success at Peachtree Alternative School.

I escorted the boys, one at a time, to the vending machine for snacks and even paid for them, myself. I was a hypocrite for buying sugary snacks. I called it a "reward for good behavior" but it was really just a time-filler.

The boys took a long time making their candy selections, which worked for me since I had run out of activities. A boy told me that he was supposed to go back to regular school but his father kept missing the enrollment meetings. Back in the classroom, the boys ate chocolate and squirmed until it was time to go outside.

Ms. Pearl was already on the field. It was cold, blustery day, and she hunched in a jacket with her arms crossed. She watched a high schooler with a buzz cut and big silver links around his neck. "I don't trust him," she said. "He's sneaky. I don't trust him, one bit.

"I wonder what'll happen to these kids when they graduate . . . *if* they graduate," she said.

"Will you take me back in?" Tom asked me. Ms. Pearl agreed to watch my charges so I followed Tom inside, where he promptly hid inside a dark closet. I handed him a bar of chocolate from my pocket, and he ate it on the floor. I was tired and wasn't inclined to move him so I stationed myself outside the door. I sat on a stool and tried to stay awake. My pregnancy made me extra sleepy. I calculated that as a substitute teacher, the school system was paying me five bucks for thirty minutes of guarding a kid in a closet.

The kids from outside wanted to go to the gym so Ms. Pearl and I traded places. She sat on my stool and I followed a group to the gymnasium. Ms. W-J and her middle schoolers were already there. "Middle school is crowded, again," she told me. "I have eighteen students in science class, and they're a handful." Coming from Ms. W-J, I knew it was an understatement.

"Can I go back to the room?" asked one of my students.

"No!" I said, fed up with moving around, based on student whims.

A couple of Mr. Martin's boys snuck out the door, and I went to retrieve them. "Can we go back to the track?" Andrew asked. I was no fan of the gymnasium. I hesitated and he took advantage of it. "Come on. Mr. Osa is out there," he said.

Students would probably go, anyway, so I relented. "Go around the building, not through it," I said, to minimize disruptions. In the parking lot, the boys started taking swings at each other. The sneaky kid with the buzz cut was the leader of the roughhousing. We were right by Ms. Bates' window. The boys hollered and wrestled roughly, while I dodged and guarded my stomach. My compassion and sense of humor completely drained away.

A boy dove into the bushes beside the track to urinate. "You'll have a lot to write about, today," Mr. Osa said, "especially with Ms. James gone."

The dismissal bell sounded. As the buses approached, the high schooler with the buzz cut jumped in front of a bus with his arms open. The bus wasn't going very fast but it was still shocking. The driver braked sharply and stomped off. "I've told you to leave my bus alone," she yelled at the kid then yelled at us teachers. "Why didn't you stop him?"

"They act fast," was all I could say.

The boy ignored the driver and tried to peel letters off the side of the bus. The driver moved towards him. "You better watch it!" she yelled.

"Get away from me! Get out of my face!" he yelled back. The driver was in the danger zone with an aggressive chronic disrupter. She was literally backing him into a corner, which was when injuries happened.

She stopped inches away from him. "This is your last warning," she shouted.

"I'm going to piss on your bus," he shouted back.

"And I'm going to make you lick it off." Inside the bus, an adult ride-along, who was paid to maintain order, actually started laughing.

I just wanted the boy to get on the bus and go home. I wanted my long day to end. The boy kicked a wheel but he did climb on board.

I stopped by the office, on my way out, and Ms. Henderson said she was pleased with the new superintendent. "He comes from a poor background," she said. "He told the students, 'If I can make it, you can, too.' They needed to hear that."

I learned that a special school board meeting about the budget was being held at the central office, that night, so I couldn't go home. I ate a vegetable plate at a nearby diner and headed for the meeting.

I sat behind the S.O.S. director, who would be advocating to keep Peachtree Alternative School open. She was busy reviewing her notes that were written on a yellow notepad. The seats in the board room filled quickly, and Ms. W-J and her husband slid in beside me. I spotted the principal and the counselor, in back, and gave them a wave. The chairman of the board banged his gavel and called the meeting to order.

The school board members, like Supreme Court justices, sat high above us. The new superintendent descended from on high and gave a presentation on the floor. He claimed that a lot of rumors had leaked out about the budget, last month. "Brainstorming leaked out. That's all it was, just brainstorming." *Now, there was an excuse if I ever heard one.* He presented the "real" budget proposal on an overhead projector.

The school board now wanted to keep all music and P.E. teachers, and Ms. W-J visibly relaxed. "It's been a hard couple of weeks," she whispered, "not knowing what was going to happen to me." Eighty-one paraprofessionals, however, would still be cut with the exception of special education paraprofessionals, who were federally-funded.

The new superintendent told us that if extra money came back to the county, things would be revived in the following order: athletic programs, the alternative school, and some paraprofessionals. I thought the talk of extra money was just a stall tactic to keep the audience from griping too much during the meeting. The odds of the alternative school being revived, next year, were slim. Besides, the good teachers would have already accepted jobs elsewhere.

Next, there was time for audience presentations but they were limited to just three minutes. A big digital clock with red numbers counted down the minutes. The S.O.S. director made a quick pitch, and her argument was economic. She pointed out that a lot of free opportunities were provided to students at Peachtree Alternative such as drug prevention education, life skills training, and parenting classes. If the school closed, the programs would end.

Ding! A bell sounded and her three minutes were up, even though she had only made one point. She was at least allowed to approach the bench and distribute a report on the advantages of the alternative school to each board member.

Next, a teacher in a track suit stepped up to the podium. She prefaced her presentation with "I will probably make some enemies, here, but . . ." and I winced. Beginning with an apology was not a good way to make a pitch. I looked at the seven board members, only one of whom was a woman, and thought that the whole process, making three-minute pitches from below, was rather humiliating. Only one board member was black, and he was also the only person under fifty.

The teacher in the track suit complained about the expensive new central office building. "We needed a new building," she said, "but we didn't need all these beautiful knickknacks." She was referring to the slick marble floor, plush carpeting, and ornate furnishings and decorations in the central office. I recalled an alternative teacher making the same complaint.

"My students are studying in trailers," said the teacher, "but we have these beautiful new things, here." She asked to see the budget for furnishing the central office, and the chairman of the board ordered a copy for her.

"Another thing," said the teacher, glancing at her paper, "some central office salaries are quite high. And do we really need to provide transportation for staff, here, and lunches for visitors? Cut out some frills rather than people!"

The teacher was brave because certain board members were known for retaliation, for arranging to have employees fired. The school board was actually under scrutiny for ethical violations by the League of Southern Schools, and tampering was one of the League's main concerns. If tampering allegations were found to be true, the school system could lose its accreditation and high school seniors, in the county, could lose their state-funded college scholarships.

The teacher's presentation was followed by a round of applause but the superintendent explained that eighty percent of education funding was salaries so the impact of cutting other things would be minimal. The teacher sat down but another angry woman, in the audience, wouldn't drop the overspending issue. "Why can't higher administrators just cut their salaries?" she shouted from her seat. "I work three jobs to make ends meet."

"You can have my hundred dollars a month," a board member quipped, to show that he was not well-paid. That was his choice, though, and he probably had further political aspirations.

"They do this because they like being in the sunlight," the superintendent joked about board members, but they were the only ones who laughed. They weren't winning over the audience but didn't care.

I noticed that the audience was primarily women. *Where were all the male child advocates?* Another woman stood up. "At a meeting in February," she said, "I heard that we spend $5000 for every regular student and $10,000 for every alternative student. Why is that? I don't think it's fair to spend so much on those kids."

"I was at the alternative school this morning," the superintendent was able to say. "We're separating out those kids for safety reasons. I don't know any other way around it."

The woman continued. "They're disruptive and rude because their parents can't control them. Parents need to pay, not me, a taxpayer." She received a loud round of applause.

"Many people agree with you," the superintendent said.

A bell rang, and the impromptu budget session ended. The board would finalize the budget, later in the week.

I headed home to check my messages. Ms. James would be out for another two days but I still hadn't heard from Mr. Martin. He was supposed to let me know whether or not he was chosen for jury duty. If he was, I'd have to substitute for him for an unspecified length of time and could even be teaching his kids for weeks. I imagined the worst case scenario, that he was chosen for the jury of a lengthy criminal trial.

My anxiety escalated as I drove winding rural roads in the dark. It could be me and the substitute parapro, for days on end. I fought back tears and hoped I could blame my emotional state on pregnancy hormones. What would I do with the boys for so long? We could only play with the parachute so many times.

At home, I barely acknowledged my husband and, instead, rooted around in our dusty attic for science supplies from my museum education days. I found jelly jars and, in desperation, decided that we would make butter. All you had to do was pour in heavy cream, add salt, and shake the jars for ten minutes. You could even do it to music. I had my husband find some good CDs. The danger was that the boys would throw the butter against the walls.

On my way to the grocery store to purchase heavy cream, I stopped by a video store for some appropriate videos. I rented enough videos for the rest of the week: *Holes, Harry Potter,* and *Pirates of the Caribbean.* By then, it was 10:00 PM, and I had worked myself into a dither. *Where was that darned Mr. Martin? Why was he stringing me along?*

He finally phoned while I was paying for groceries, saying he'd been lifting weights at the gym. It turned out that he wasn't chosen for jury duty, after all.

"I heard things went pretty well, today," he said.

By what standard? Who was he kidding? A kid had jumped in front of a school bus!

"Well, Andrew threatened to throw a chair a couple of times," I reported, "and Tom climbed into the rafters." I'd almost forgotten about those incidents. A thunderstorm began, as I drove home, and the heavy cream leaked in my car.

Chapter 10

May

MAY 7

The department chair was vague when she booked me as a "floating substitute" so I was unsure of my responsibilities. "This is going to be horrible," I told my husband as I headed out the front door. I arrived at the school at 7:45 AM and was thrilled to see another substitute in the department chair's room, instead of me. Maybe I wouldn't be needed, after all. The young woman behind the teacher's desk wore a pink shirt, which made her look even younger.

I tried to find the special ed. department chair who was somewhere in the building, doing lesson planning. "Where are you, today?" Ms. Henderson barked at me in her principal's voice.

"I thought I was supposed to be in special education but there's already a sub, in there."

Ms. Bates overheard and suggested I sub for her while she attended Teacher Appreciation Day activities. It was Teacher Appreciation Day across the country, and teachers at Peachtree Alternative would receive gifts and be treated to a special lunch. Ms. Henderson wanted to know exactly whom I was subbing for so she wouldn't have to pay me, needlessly.

Ms. Bates accompanied me on my search for the special ed. department chair. She looked at the crowds of students in the halls and said she was ready for school to end. "Especially since it's the last year," she said. "There's a different feel in the air."

We ran into the department chair, who promptly told Ms. Bates, "Mary's pregnant so we have to take it easy on her." I didn't argue, and the two women agreed that a substitute was needed to help run the book fair. That was right up my alley, and I hurried to the library.

Figure 10.   Crime Scene Tape in the Gymnasium.

Ms. Hackett's book fair was open to parents, students, and teachers. All teachers had received fifteen dollar gift certificates to spend on books. I straightened displays of young adult novels and thought it was a much better task than handling belligerent teenagers. I recommended books to kids and supervised the high schoolers who were manning the cash register.

It was a big book fair sponsored by a major publisher, and there were many good titles. I enjoyed talking about literature with Ms. Hackett. She had run the book fair for three years in a row and, last year, she earned $5000 for Peachtree Alternative.

The irony of Teacher Appreciation Day was that most teachers appeared to be having a really rotten time. From my vantage point in the centrally located library, I could see their haggard faces, clearly. Special education students wandered the halls, and their belabored teachers scurried behind them. Mr. Martin followed a student who refused to return to the classroom, and Mr. Osa did the same thing, although he finally resorted to grabbing the kid by the collar. The young substitute in pink yelled at a group of boys loitering in the hall, "Hey! Get back here!"

"How are you doing?" I asked the young woman.

To my surprise, she said, "It's better than subbing at Franklin Middle School, any day."

Ms. James came in to use her gift certificate and looked wan despite her deep tan. She wore a pained expression, as she tried to keep a kid from stealing a book.

Smoke billowed in from where Mr. Martin was grilling hot dogs for a teachers' cookout. The feast was served in a conference room. The hugging paraprofessional had lined the walls with big black-and-white photographs of all the staff, and I was touched to see my own image.

After school, I tracked down the department chair and made a point of thanking her for my gentle day in the library.

MAY 17

Mr. Owens's second period history class had reached the twenty-first century. "What happened in the year 2000?" he asked students as he stood by the board.

"I don't know," snapped a churlish girl in front.

"Nothing's really sticking out," said a boy behind her.

"I'll start," said Mr. Owens. He began a list with "Y2K, voting problems, Elian Gonzales, and KURSK." He elaborated on the KURSK, the sunken Russian submarine, which was vivid to him as a former navy seaman.

"Why are we even talking about this?" the churlish girl asked.

"Because it's American history class, Amy," said Mr. Owens, with an edge to his voice. "Even though the KURSK is not American history, it still affected us."

The standard shouting came from Mr. Wilson's math class. Still, some of the kids in our room managed to sleep. A line of boys slumped against a wall, beneath their hoods, while Mr. Owens taught the handful of kids who were listening. Two surfer-type boys, in shell necklaces, bent their heads together and worked on an art project.

A student reminded Mr. Owens of the American submarine that surfaced into a Japanese fishing vessel, killing nine people. Two immature boys in the room snickered, but Mr. Owens didn't hear them. He explained that the accident was caused by civilians, who were "blowing" the submarine steeply to the surface. "I've done it a hundred times, myself," Mr. Owens said.

"What angle is it?" asked a boy.

"Almost straight up," said Mr. Owens. "It would be so steep that your hand would be on the floor." He added more events to the list on the board then asked if everyone had copied the information. I was the only person in the room with a pen poised but Mr. Owens erased the board, anyway.

"If I asked you to summarize the twenty-first century, what would you say?" he asked.

"I wouldn't say anything," said the churlish girl but Mr. Owens just ignored her. She flicked a sleeping boy on the ear, several times, with a long fingernail.

"Don't blame yourselves for not recalling current events, right away," Mr. Owens said. "We do history, chronologically, but current events, by subject matter. We need something to spark our memories."

He continued with his reassurance. "Even if you fail the final exam," he said, "don't think you don't know anything about American history. We've learned a lot of things, in here, things that even adults don't know."

As we headed for lunch, I asked Mr. Owens where he would be next year. He was going to teach state history at a brand new middle school, in Peachtree County, and he was pretty excited about it. According to Mr. Owens, a lot of people wanted to teach state history. The competition was stiff. He, himself, had wanted to teach it since he first began teaching five years ago, and he had certainly paid his dues.

"I've immersed myself in local history wherever I've lived," he told me. "I studied Florida history when I lived in Florida and Vermont history when I lived there but this is my home state. I have all kinds of contacts, here, relatives in historical societies and friends in museums." He was already planning field trips for next year. He wanted to give students guided tours of historic sites.

The state flag had changed, over the years, and Mr. Owens planned to purchase the different versions, with his own money, and string them across the ceiling of his new classroom.

"Ms. Bates said I've been extra quiet, lately," Mr. Owens told me. "I think it's because I'm trying to distance myself from this school. It's how I'm coping. I'm not happy about leaving these students, but I'm happy about a new classroom.

"Ms. Bates is the best partner I've had at any job and I'll miss her, but I'm looking forward to working with new people and getting fresh ideas."

At lunch, Mr. Owens ate half a steak that he brought from home. A former student, who now worked at a butcher shop, always gave him a special discount on meat. I learned that the math teacher would also be going to the new middle school, and Ms. Bates would teach English at Holly Springs High School. Ms. Wilkins would give up her academic counseling responsibilities and would return to teaching English at Franklin High School.

When I visited 200 Hall, I heard that special education would remain at Peachtree Alternative, next year. The special education students would just be ghosts, flitting through abandoned hallways. The picture grew grimmer as Ms. James worried about next year's meals. "The cafeteria will be closed. What are we going to eat?" she asked.

"Sack lunches, every day," I joked, although it was probably true.

"See? What did I tell you?" Ms. James said to Ms. Singh. "They're going to feed us baloney, all week."

I passed Mr. Osa's class and saw he had a substitute teacher. Students were fighting in the doorway of his room. One boy shoved the door open while another tried to slam it closed.

Ms. Pearl, who rarely yelled, was yelling at another student who was running away, down the hall. She also yelled at a student who was spinning in an office chair. Mark, from Mr. Osa's room, was leaving the building with his mother. "I should press charges against that kid for slapping me," I heard him say. They were snapshots of disorder.

I joined a group of four girls waiting to get inside the gym. "Is someone coming with a key?" I asked and got a churlish response.

"No, we're just standing here for the fun of it," said a girl.

Ms. W-J came with the key, and the crowd behind her swelled to a whopping thirty-one students. Deputy Rodriguez patrolled the fringes of the crowd. He deposited the kids but didn't stay.

"I'm not putting up with any funny business," Ms. W-J announced before unlocking the doors but there was fun aplenty. A corner of the gymnasium had been marked off with yellow crime tape. Equipment had been vandalized, although it was rather hard to tell, since it was old to begin with. The crime scene tape was a magnet for students, and Ms. W-J grew hoarse from telling kids to stay away. "Get away from the tape," she yelled over and over, and my head began to throb.

Ms. W-J held her two-way radio aloft with one hand, a defensive posture signaling to students that she could call for help at any minute. She actually did have to call the deputy because someone stole a Gameboy from her purse while she pursued a kid across the floor. Her purse was sitting right next to me on the bleachers. A few students had come over to ask me the time but I certainly hadn't seen anyone swipe anything. "This the first time, all year, this has happened to me," Ms. W-J said about the theft.

"I can't believe I didn't see anything," I told her.

"They're slick," said Ms. W-J.

She was going to be a physical education teacher at the new Franklin High School, next year. It would have a brand new sports complex. After a decade in a decrepit building, Ms. W-J deserved to work in a sparkling new gymnasium.

At the end of the day, I visited the art teacher, who was in her room sorting supplies. She grinned widely as she told me that, next year, she would be the art teacher at a new middle school. "No more having a room without a sink," she said.

MAY 22

A pizza delivery man brought eighty-nine pizzas to the school. Ms. Wilkins and a pizza executive doled out slices to hungry students. Teachers were in a jolly mood on the last day of school, and students could leave after lunch, with parental permission.

Eight pizzas had been set aside for the staff. I chose some slices and sat across from the middle school teachers. Betty, the cafeteria manager, teased Ms. Cox. "You won't know how to handle regular kids."

"Oh, yes I will," the art teacher shot back.

Betty looked at the rowdy students in the cafeteria and shook her head. She had already chewed some of them out for jumping on a table. "I can't imagine all these kids loose in the summer," she said. "What's going to happen? They'll probably go to jail."

There were no tears or presents on the last day of Peachtree Alternative School, although I did spot one mature boy shaking Mr. Owens's hand. Kids just hurried away.

I watched a gang of four boys lope across the street. One boy removed his white t-shirt and wrapped it around his head like a turban. His blue jean shorts hung well below his boxers. School was out, and he raised his fists overhead in a gesture of triumph.

MAY 25

I arrived ten minutes early to the goodbye luncheon at Peachtree Alternative School but tables were already filled. Ms. Pearl showed up in shorts and sneakers. She took one peek in the door and hurried home to change clothes for the fancy occasion.

The lights were low, and tables were covered in white tablecloths and votive candles. Metallic confetti was sprinkled all around. Soft jazz played over some speakers, and the walls were decorated with multicolored stars. A program at each place setting read "A Farewell to Peachtree Alternative School."

The principal escorted me to a table labeled "support staff," and I overheard a teacher saying, "This lunchroom has never looked better." There were also tables for parole officers, the sheriff's department, business partners, volunteers, and central office personnel. The room was brimming with friends of the school. Ms. Henderson and Ms. Wilkins sat at a head table beside a podium. Also up front was a round table covered with awards.

We lined up for the buffet. Betty's wonderful spread consisted of pot roast, baked chicken, rice, broccoli, homemade rolls, green beans, and seven-layer salad. I loaded my plate and returned to my seat beside one of the school's former assistant principals.

The man reminisced about his old job. "I had to be creative about disciplining kids, here," the former assistant principal said. He was also a former ROTC instructor, and he had just returned from active duty in Iraq.

I could not imagine the soft-spoken man, beside me, issuing orders but one thing my year at Peachtree Alternative School had taught me was to never underestimate anyone. Looks could be deceiving. I spotted the pretty parole officers in sleeveless dresses at a table filled with burly men. They defied stereotypes, as did the gentle Ms. Bates, the slender special ed. department chair, and tiny Ms. Singh. They were a far cry from the Rambo-like teachers that I once thought were standard in alternative schools.

Only one board member sat at the central office table, and I wondered if she felt awkward being there, since the school board was responsible for shutting the place down. Three board members were already planning to resign, in light of tampering allegations. The men had paved the way for their resignations by saying they needed to "spend more time with their families."

We finished eating, and the presentation began. The theme of the luncheon was a kaleidoscope, and representatives from the school stood up and presented a variety of colored ribbons. Ms. W-J, who had been at Peachtree Alternative since its doors opened, won a gold ribbon for Outstanding Middle School Teacher.

"She has the wisdom of a hundred years," the presenter said about Ms. W-J, and the audience laughed. "She always has a kind word for students and nothing ruffles her feathers."

Ms. Bates presented a blue ribbon for Outstanding High School Teacher. "Blue is an appropriate color for the high school," she said. "It's the color of the sea. Sometimes, the waters have been calm. Sometimes, they've been choppy and, sometimes, they've been in turmoil. Mostly, they've been calm.

"Students don't stand a chance with us high school teachers," she told the audience, "We're a team. We're a family. Mr. Owens is our big brother, Mr. Wilson is our crazy uncle, and I'm the mom." She presented a blue ribbon to the computer teacher for his multiple roles as teacher, advisor, and technology expert.

Mr. Martin was next to approach the podium. "The color for special education is hot pink," he said. "We chose hot pink, as our color, because our emotions are close to the surface. When things are rough, we keep on going." The department chair was awarded a hot pink ribbon for Outstanding Special Educator and she received a hug from Mr. Martin.

Ms. Wilkins named members of the community who had been supportive of the school, over the years, including ministers, substance abuse counselors, social workers, and judges. "We've been the envy of many alternative programs," she said, "because of all our community support. So many alternative schools have to struggle for it. We're privileged to have a fine support system."

A local newspaper reporter, who sometimes wrote about the school, and a food and nutrition volunteer were also acknowledged. "You wouldn't think big, old teens would want to learn about nutrition," said Ms. Wilkins, "but, let me tell you, they play a vicious game of vegetable jeopardy." Finally, she awarded a light blue ribbon to the Save Our Students director for Outstanding Community Support.

Ms. Wilkins was on the verge of tears. She was one of the original founders of the school, and it was hard for her to say goodbye. "I'm a dramatic person," she told us, sniffling. "I'm trying not to be dramatic but I want you to know . . ." she pointed to the wall behind her. "See all those stars? For the last ten years, you've been stars in the theater of my heart." She choked up and sat down.

The part-time nurse, custodians, school psychologist, and cafeteria staff were also recognized. I didn't even know the school had a psychologist but the older woman with wild, frizzy hair looked vaguely familiar. I may have seen her in the front office behind tall stacks of papers.

The math teacher presented a purple ribbon to Mr. Johnson, the custodian on 100 Hall, and teased him by saying, "I tried to take away his radio so Ms. Henderson wouldn't bother him but he wouldn't let me."

The special education department chair thanked the parole and security officers. All of the men from the sheriff's department were wearing casual uniforms, and they looked nice in khaki pants and olive polo shirts. "They're considered tough guys," the department chair said, "but we see beyond that. We see them in action: giving smiles, pats on the back, and high fives. They're respectful, honest, and really care about kids." The table of officers received a hearty round of applause.

Ms. Hackett thanked the school business partners, including a bank, a local trucking company, a restaurant, and a superstore. The partners provided money for field trips and other special events and cash incentives to students. "We have a caring community," Ms. Hackett said. "Without them, we wouldn't have a school."

The big awards, lighthouse awards, came next. They were actually miniature lighthouses, which was an appropriate metaphor for people who were beacons to teens. The cafeteria manager won a lighthouse award for planning so many good meals.

Mr. Owens won Teacher of the Year. "He's an innovative teacher who reaches the most difficult students," Ms. Bates said about her friend. "He's calm and greets them with a smile. We'll miss this exceptional teacher."

Over at the head table, Ms. Wilkins took off her glasses and dabbed her eyes. She couldn't stem the flow of tears, though, and put her head in her hands and her shoulders shook. The army veteran beside me started sniffing.

The ceremony began to wind down, and Ms. Henderson was the last person to speak. "I spent all my budget money on this luncheon so a donation cup will be by the door," she joked. "Staff members, here, have served and served and served some more. Thank you from the very bottom of my heart."

She gave Ms. Bates a lighthouse award for Outstanding Service as chair of the alternative high school. "She believes students can succeed," said Ms. Henderson, "and she doesn't know how to say 'no.'"

The principal gave another lighthouse award for Outstanding Service to Ms. Hackett for organizing field trips, fundraisers, and the goodbye luncheon. "She always gives 500%," said Ms. Henderson. "She works well with our exceptional students and is a liaison with our partners."

Finally, a lighthouse award for resiliency went to Ms. Wilkins. "I look for her red truck, every morning, when I come to school," said the principal. "She calls me 'sunshine' and I call her 'rainbow.' She calls the middle schoolers 'popcorn kids' because they're so lively. She believes we can save every student." The biggest of lighthouse of all went to Ms. Wilkins.

"Today is different," said the principal. "The majority of staff in this room have been reassigned." She mustered a final plea. "Don't ever, ever give up on these kids because we won't."

Epilogue

Several years later, I tracked down as many former Peachtree Alternative School teachers as I could find. They were very successful in regular public schools, which was hardly surprising, given the high quality of their work and their experience levels. They had cut their teeth on alternative students.

Ms. Pearl and Ms. Wilkins went on to win awards at their new schools: Support Person of the Year and Teacher of the Year. Ms. Bates earned an additional teaching certificate in gifted education and taught all of her classes at Holly Springs High School at a gifted level, even her regular and remedial classes. She also completed all of her coursework for a doctorate and was finishing her dissertation. When I asked Ms. Bates how she managed to do so much, she laughed and told me that she would probably drop dead on the classroom floor from overworking and that she would have to live to be 150 to fit everything in.

Ms. W-J had a second child and was enjoying a vast new gymnasium at the new Franklin High School, which was complete with skylights and an indoor track. She taught health and physical education and everyone, at the larger school, called her "Coach." In another new school, Ms. Cox had a much larger art room. She had big closets, sturdy new tables, and several sinks. There was plenty of space to display student quilts, pottery, and folk art. Upstairs at Martin Middle School, her colleague Mr. Owens kept on dazzling students with spellbinding lessons. He had earned his Master's degree and continued to serve as an unofficial building disciplinarian. If a fight broke out, female teachers ran all the way down the hall, past other male teachers, just to get him.

Ms. Henderson served as an assistant principal at a regular high school in a neighboring county, before retiring. She was bored in retirement, though,

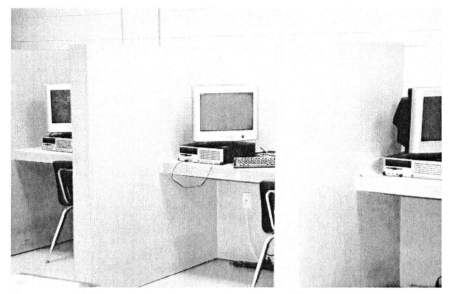

Figure 11.   Cubicles at the New Computer Center for At-risk Youth in Peachtree County.

and accepted another difficult position. She replaced a principal who was murdered in a non-school-related incident.

The Peachtree County School Board was investigated by the regional accreditation agency, and board members were found guilty of tampering for inappropriately hiring and promoting their friends. The county school system was put on probation for a year. The following year, the county schools developed new hiring protocols and the sanction was downgraded to a warning but was not lifted, altogether. The accreditation agency found ongoing tampering on the part of one board member, whose name was not released to the public.

The alternative school in Peachtree County was replaced by a computer center. At-risk youth visited the center in the mornings or afternoons for computer self-instruction. The facility that housed the computer center was badly damaged one summer by four teenaged vandals. They smashed computers, spray-painted desks, and used a podium as a battering ram. More distressing news emerged later. A teacher at the computer center was arrested for child pornography and his school computer was confiscated by state investigators.

Some former Peachtree Alternative students went on to graduate from high school. Heather graduated and drove all the way to Ms. Cox's house to deliver a thank you note and flowers. Ms. Cox said that Heather was the only alternative student who ever visited her home.

Mr. Owens reported that he often saw former students working in stores, and he marveled at their gratitude. Some of them gave him big hugs. He kept an eye on the police blotter, though. Two former Peachtree Alternative students were in jail for murder and one was on the county's Ten Most Wanted list.

Author's Note: Reflections on Alternative Schooling

My year at Peachtree Alternative School mostly reinforced what I already knew about good teaching of students in poverty and good teaching in general. As a college professor at the University of Alabama-Birmingham, I often began my graduate classes by defining quality teaching. I liked to introduce a small book called *The Elements of Teaching* by James Banner and Harold Cannon.

The authors clearly and succinctly identify elements such as enthusiasm, authority, humility, creativity, and authenticity as critical aspects of teaching. By authority, they mean substantial knowledge about one's subject, and by authenticity, they mean being oneself in the classroom. Banner and Cannon emphasize that there is no one model of a good teacher. Good teachers can be young or old, big or small, stern or relaxed, serious or humorous.

The Teacher of the Year at Peachtree Alternative School embodied all of their elements. Mr. Owens's enthusiasm was usually contagious enough to win over even the strongest resisters. He was a walking encyclopedia and was unflinchingly honest and always open to advice. He had creative plans for field trips and decorating his classroom by stringing state flags across the ceiling. No one was more down-to-earth and calm, as his own students pointed out, and the man was wonderfully eccentric. I only wish that I could have seen him, in his younger days, with his white Mohawk hairdo and combat boots. Banner and Cannon caution that only a paragon meets all of their criteria but, in my mind, Mr. Owens comes close.

Mr. Owens had a habit of approaching every new group of students as a genuine, open person who respected them, not as a distant and disapproving authority figure. In my entire career, I have never seen a first day class as successful as Mr. Owens's at Peachtree Alternative School. The audible, collective sigh of satisfaction that I heard at the end of his first class meeting, during second semester, was amazing, palpable, and something that all teachers should strive for. To this day, I hear observers rave about Mr. Owens's first day classes.

I once had the good fortune of meeting author James Loewan, who wrote *Lies My Teacher Told Me: Everything American History Textbooks Got Wrong,* when he gave a presentation at the University of Cincinnati. James Loewan would be proud of Mr. Owens, if he met him. The Teacher of the Year went far beyond the dry history textbook. He enlivened history lessons with photographs of child labor and Civil War artifacts. He mesmerized students with accounts of his submarine days and presented topics that were inherently interesting. The alternative students, most of whom were poor, could relate to the social injustices and oppression he presented. He connected historic events to contemporary life and was a superb storyteller. Mr. Owens also urged students to question what they read, not take everything at face value, and not be too judgmental.

Another author, Martin Haberman, specifically identifies the ideologies of star teachers of children in poverty. His research is primarily set in poor urban communities, but poor rural communities have some of the same problems, these days, although they are probably not as extreme. Gangs predominate, unemployment is high, and drug problems are rampant in both communities. There are dying textile towns beside railroads in rural areas, just as there are dying steel industries in cities.

I saw Haberman's ideologies of star teachers of children in poverty reflected in the behaviors of teachers at Peachtree Alternative School. Foremost was respect for both parents and students. Ms. Henderson was respectful of parents when she urged teachers to call them, early in the year, with good news. The academic counselor was respectful in her gentle handling of the parent who was a former felon with "H-A-T-E" on his knuckles. She apologized for embarrassing him and even suggested that he work in her home.

Coach W-J was always professional and ever respectful of students, and they responded accordingly. At the final banquet, where she won Outstanding Middle School Teacher, she was described as someone who always had a kind word for students. In fact, I never heard her say anything unkind about anyone. She remains one of my personal role models.

The star teachers at Peachtree Alternative School also demonstrated Haberman's inherent faith in young people, exemplified by such public statements as Ms. Cox's "These are good kids. They're good kids. They just haven't made good choices," and Ms. Hackett's "This is someplace you grow to love and you're here because you want to be here. We even have gifted kids. These kids aren't so bad. They're just kids who've made mistakes, and some have only made one mistake." Mr. Owens also told alternative students that he was fiercely proud of them. Although the reality is you can't save every child, it is wonderful that Ms. Wilkins still reaches for the stars and believes otherwise, as stated by the principal at the final banquet.

An alternative school is not the place for anyone who is zealous, inflexible, or egotistical. It is a place for people who can admit their mistakes. Haberman is absolutely emphatic about the importance of teachers of children in poverty admitting their mistakes. Children make mistakes and at-risk youth make many mistakes; therefore, alternative school teachers should certainly be able to admit their own. I remember Ms. Wilkins sparring with Miranda, the girl in the black bra and sheer top, then confessing, "I guess I made things worse." Later, Ms. Bates repaired another mistake with Miranda by asking the girl about her hard day, providing one-on-one attention, and modifying an assignment that was confusing to Miranda, as a new student. I saw a lot of humanity and admissions of fallibility during my year at Peachtree Alternative School, and they are major hallmarks of good teaching.

From Peachtree Alternative School teachers, I learned about forgiving students . . . forgiving them for making your days so difficult and for bigger things such as assault. Ms. Cox, Ms. Bates, Ms. Singh, and the Special Ed. Department Chair all forgave students after being shoved, hit with a book, threatened with a makeshift weapon, and hit with a heavy metal trashcan. Not holding grudges is difficult for many adults, but it is monumentally important for alternative school teachers.

In *Star Teachers of Children in Poverty,* Martin Haberman also writes that stars must have outside interests so they won't burn out. Stars are well-rounded and mentally stable people, and Peachtree Alternative teachers certainly illustrated this. Ms. Cox went home, at night, and made jewelry and pottery. Ms. Hackett scouted out garage sales, in her spare time. Ms. W-J lifted weights and, of course, Mr. Owens was immersed in reenacting. Ms. Bates was busy with her husband, kids, and grandkids, and Ms. Henderson went antiquing, on weekends, and volunteered at a local night shelter. Many Peachtree Alternative teachers were regular churchgoers. The star educators at the school were sustained by their hobbies, friends, family, and spirituality. Taking time for oneself, time to recover from the stresses of the classroom, is a lesson that many overachieving, beginning teachers still need to learn.

High expectations were common at Peachtree Alternative School. From a messy art project using black paint to a chemical reaction lesson involving explosions to poetry analysis, I experienced high expectations across the disciplines, and teachers retained them in their new workplaces. Over and over, again, in my years as an educator, I have seen students rise to meet the high expectations of dedicated and determined teachers. It is the premiere way to teach.

The star educators at Peachtree Alternative School also pursued highly creative projects, which they didn't have to fight for because Ms. Henderson was so tolerant. Her openness was even emphasized during my job interview. Ms. Bates did poetry projects, Ms. Cox did scratch-outs, and Ms. W-J built volcanoes. Ms. Hackett brought a park ranger with a hawk to school then she brought a goat. Ms. Henderson even let Mr. Owens take a break for reenacting in Florida, a supreme act of faith on the part of an understanding principal.

Not only was Ms. Hackett a creative paraprofessional, she was also an extraordinarily hard worker, who was most deserving of an Outstanding Service Award. The discussion of the Civil Rights Movement that she led with special education middle schoolers (a very difficult group at Peachtree Alternative) was so powerful that it raised chill bumps on our arms. Thrilling moments at the circus were also courtesy of Ms. Hackett, who constantly solicited donations and partner involvement.

As far as the school buildings went, I had some grave concerns. The decrepit facility with its waterless gymnasium, dark abandoned hallway, boarded up windows, and collapsing ceiling always reminded me of the crumbling schools depicted in Jonathan Kozol's *Savage Inequalities: Children in America's Schools.*

As for the school location, rural Franklin was not the worst place for an alternative school. Peachtree Alternative School could have been even more deeply isolated in a rural community and devoid of connections to hardworking adult role models, therefore, much more dangerous. Instead, the school was just minutes from the county sheriff's department and was an easy drive for community advocates.

New knowledge that I gained at Peachtree Alternative School was the concept of not fighting back. Ginger Rhode, William Jensen, and C. Reavis, authors of *The Tough Kid Book,* advise teachers who work with chronically disruptive students to never confront them. According to the authors, such students are masters of confrontation and will always win. Teachers must conserve their energy for the rest of the class. At Peachtree Alternative School, I learned that redirecting, deflecting, and defusing anger are much better techniques than confrontation. Distraction, using humor, and saying "I'm sorry you feel that way but . . ." are now part of my teaching toolkit.

At first, I thought that nonconfrontation was cowardly but I quickly saw the wisdom of it. Most alternative teachers agreed wholeheartedly with nonconfrontation. Ms. Bates even told me a somber tale about the time she literally backed a student into a corner and he returned, the next day, with a gun. Fortunately, the gun was intercepted before he could use it. I remember being shocked when Ms. Singh chose to ignore a student, who was poised to stab her in the forehead. Similarly, the special education department chair (another savvy woman with a decade of experience at the school) gave up and let the very same student go to the gym rather than push him too far. Now, I know that successful alternative school teachers exercise a type of self-preservative common sense.

In *How to Establish an Alternative School,* John Kellmayer makes the extraordinary claim that, in his many years in alternative schools, he has never raised his voice with a student. (Mr. Owens once told me the very same thing about himself.) Kellmayer rationalizes that if he never raises his voice and can be counted on to remain calm, students will be more willing to come to him when they are in serious trouble.

For nonexceptional teachers, I think that nonconfrontation, nonretaliation, and gentleness are behaviors that take practice. I lost my own temper and yelled at alternative students, particularly in the spring, even though I knew better. I am determined to remain calm in future stressful teaching situations.

Some ethical dilemmas still haunt me. I probably should have reported Mike, the kid who bragged about his whiskey and .38 Special, to his parole officer. Without much reflection, I made a quick note and kept going. One thing that can be said of long bouts of careful observation is that they are exhausting. I sometimes wrote field notes then promptly forgot them. Mike ended up in youth detention, just weeks later, for failing a drug test, and no one knows where he is now.

I cannot, in good conscience, end this book without addressing the most difficult issue brought to light . . . solitary confinement. At the time, I did not press people about the policy. I was too shaken by my discovery of the cell.

I did press educators, years later, and what I found was denial or uneasy acceptance. I already knew that the computer teacher was in denial when he told me, "I don't go back there."

There were a couple of other classrooms, in the building, that were not part of Peachtree Alternative School or even the county school system. They were used by Chambers Psychoeducational Center for students who were even more emotionally and behaviorally disturbed than alternative students. Chambers was a state-funded center. I did not visit the psychoeducational classrooms, at the end of 200 Hall, because they were not, technically, part of the alternative school.

Most teachers, whose rooms were not near the cell, thought that it was just Chambers students who had been wrestled into the hole. That was not the case. Even some teachers who were closer to the cell still thought (or told themselves) that it was Chambers students who were being confined.

Those teachers who had been directly involved knew otherwise. They were able to justify solitary confinement, somewhat, by telling themselves it was a last resort for students who were endangering themselves and others.

I saw that confinement troubled adults, severely. They were distressed, defensive, close-mouthed, even sick, when it happened. I, myself, had the extreme physical reaction of nausea.

I also have a hard time comprehending solitary confinement in light of the mostly therapeutic techniques that I witnessed, such as field trips, creative projects, and service opportunities. From my perspective, solitary confinement is an example of how even good people in alternative schools can stand back and let bad things happen. In extreme conditions, they follow the rules or resort to apathy, just like disaffected youth in their own classrooms. And I have no doubt that putting a young person into a cell inside a public school building is wrong.

If public school students are dangerous enough to be put in solitary confinement, they are dangerous enough to be removed from the building. Extraction of aggressive students should be immediate, and well-trained personnel should be available to do it. No teacher, substitute, paraprofessional, or administrator should ever have to think about removing a child's jacket and shoelaces so he won't hang himself in solitary confinement!

Isolation cubbies, waterless gymnasiums, and solitary confinement cells are where I draw the line.

On a lighter note, the power of children's literature continues to sustain me, and it was prominent in the curriculum at Peachtree Alternative School. As the child of a children's literature teacher, books have always been a valuable part of my life. Authors such as Ashley Bryan, Christopher Paul Curtis, Louis Sachar, Richard Peck, and Barbara Robinson are heroes to me. Robinson, the creator of the Horrible Herdman characters, was probably the funniest author that I ever read as a child. It was a privilege to share Barbara Robinson's work with my friend Jarrod. Richard Peck, whom I read as an adult, is a close second for the all-time funniest children's author. The same can be said for humorous children's authors such as Christopher Paul Curtis and Louis Sachar, who manage to weave important historical and contemporary lessons into their comic tales.

I will never forget Ashley Bryan melting the audience of hard-core teenagers at Peachtree Alternative School. Ms. Pearl's delight and students' awe were evident in their smiles, amen's, and open mouths. Those emotions, plus Mr. Martin's silent congratulatory rapping, were all special to me. To be in the presence of such a wise and generous man as Ashley Bryan was meaningful to all of us.

Ashley's personal advice, to me, to not respond to chronically disruptive students with anger was born of his own experience at the Wiltwyck School for

Boys in the 1960s. His advice echoes that of Martin Haberman, who promotes gentle teaching. Ashley Bryan, with his kindly presence, embodies this belief, as do Mr. Owens, Ms. Bates, Ms.W-J, and other Peachtree Alternative teachers.

One of the biggest errors that the Peachtree County School Board made was eliminating the school librarian position. The vast majority of alternative students have poor literacy skills, and they need access to a library with a specialist to guide them. Allowing free reading time and a choice of reading, as in Ms. Bates's class, is also very important. Ms. Bates role modeled appreciation for reading by letting students catch her reading a good book in her spare time. Ms. Hackett also loved literature and successfully taught poetry in her own very challenging classroom. She went above and beyond the call of duty to hold an annual book fair at the school.

Reading aloud to students, with enthusiasm, is another way to hook them. As I learned at Peachtree Alternative School, students who feign indifference may, in fact, be listening and you can't always tell how many words actually sink in.

Beyond a love of books and a love of learning, another thing that sustained me and many teachers at Peachtree Alternative School was humor. The principal even told me about humor as a coping mechanism on Day Two, saying, "I have to laugh or else I'd go crazy." The humor, in the school, was a gallows humor, akin to that of doctors and nurses in emergency rooms, but it was humor none the less. In their lowest moments, upon learning of the school's imminent closure, teachers coped by making wisecracks about prostitution and retaliation.

Ms. Bates's wry sense of humor was apparent, even years later, in her jokes about overworking and aging. She even joked about classroom management in her new regular school. Her regular students knew that she spent years teaching at an alternative school and, as Ms. Bates put it, they lived in fear of her bringing out a whip or a stun gun. She teased me by saying that she coped with bad days at the alternative school by drinking Friday night margaritas then, seriously, told me it was great colleagues like Mr. Owens who kept her going.

Sometimes the antics of alternative students were so outrageous that there was nothing to do *but* laugh. Stealing fishhooks, urinating in public, climbing the rafters . . . the list goes on.

I have come full circle. I began with Haberman's philosophy of education and ended with it. I finished a year in a tough school, not as a teacher, as I originally planned, but as a substitute and a family member. I began with Ms. Henderson's words, "These are tough kids," and ended with her advice, "Don't ever, ever give up on these kids because we won't."

The answer to chronically disruptive students in our public schools is not confinement. It is not boot camps and it is certainly not computer self-instruction, in which unmotivated students are expected to motivate themselves, devoid of relationships with teachers. That solution is so absurd as to almost be laughable. Computers are lifeless, and cubicles foster sensory deprivation.

The solution to chronically disruptive youth is, ironically, the exact opposite of confinement. It is freedom. It is freedom of choice and movement (within certain boundaries) that is guided by creative, compassionate, healthy adults who facilitate last-ditch learning. Let us embody the ideologies of star teachers and embrace the therapeutic philosophy of alternative schooling and wholeheartedly pursue it.

Bibliography

Banner, James, and Cannon, Harold (1997). *The Elements of Teaching*. New Haven, CT: Yale University Press.

Bryan, Ashley (2003). *Beautiful Blackbird*. New York: Atheneum.

Cooper, Susan (1999). *The Dark is Rising*. New York: Simon & Schuster.

Curtis, Christopher Paul (1997). *The Watsons Go to Birmingham – 1963*. New York: Random House.

Fluegelman, Andrew [Ed.] (1976). *The New Games Book*. New York: Broadway.

Going, K.L. (2003). *Fat Kid Rules the World*. New York: Penguin.

Goodman, Greg (1999). *Alternatives in Education: Critical Pedagogy for Disaffected Youth*. New York: Peter Lang.

Gruwell, Erin (1999). *The Freedom Writers Diary: How a Teacher and 150 Teens Used Writing to Change the World Around Them*. New York: Broadway.

Haberman, Martin (1995). *Star Teachers of Children in Poverty*. Indianapolis, IN: Kappa Delta Pi.

Hinton, S.E. (1967). *The Outsiders*. New York: Viking.

Horwitz, Tony (1999). *Confederates in the Attic: Dispatches from the Unfinished Civil War*. New York: Random House.

Hugo, Victor, and Wynne-Jones, Tim (Adapted by). (1997). *The Hunchback of Notre Dame*. New York: Scholastic.

Johnston, Michael (2003). *In the Deep Heart's Core*. New York: Grove Atlantic.

Kellmayer, John (1995). *How to Establish an Alternative School*. Thousand Oaks, CA: Corwin.

Kozol, Jonathan (1992). *Savage Inequalities: Children in America's Schools*. New York: HarperCollins.

Kramer, Edith (1958). *Art Therapy in a Children's Community*. Springfield, IL: Charles C. Thomas.

Lee, Raymond (1994). *Dangerous Fieldwork*. Thousand Oaks, CA: Sage.

Loewen, James (1995). *Lies My Teacher Told Me: Everything Your American History Textbook Got Wrong.* New York: Simon & Schuster.

Miller, Arthur (1976). *The Crucible: A Play in Four Acts.* New York: Penguin Play Series.

O'Brien, Robert (1987). *Z for Zachariah.* New York: Simon & Schuster.

Peck, Richard (2000). *A Long Way from Chicago.* New York: Penguin.

Rhode, Ginger, William, Jensen, and H. Kenton Reavis (1993). *The Tough Kid Book: Practical Classroom Management Strategies.* Frederick, CO: Sopris West.

Robinson, Barbara, and Brown, Judith (Illustrator) (1972). *The Best Christmas Pageant Ever.* New York: HarperCollins.

Sachar, Louis (2000). *Holes.* New York: Random House.

Sinclair, Upton (1989). *The Jungle (Penguin Classics Series).* New York: Penguin.

Spinelli, Jerry (1999). *Maniac Magee.* New York: Little, Brown, & Company.

Steinbeck, John (1947). *The Pearl.* New York: Penguin.

Index

ADHD. *See* Attention Deficit
   Hyperactivity Disorder
Alexander, Lloyd, 11
Antigua, 64
Arkansas, 4, 11
arson, 25, 44, 47
art education, 21–23, 117-18, 157, 163
assault, 46–47, 58, 67, 69–70, 73, 105,
   108
Atlanta, Georgia, 9, 29
Attention Deficit Hyperactivity
   Disorder (ADHD), 43, 112
autism, 43

baggy pants, 15–16, 27, 34, 49, 81, 97,
   158
basketball, 19, 24, 25, 43, 49, 81, 92
Birmingham Civil Rights Institute, 139
Black American spirituals, vii, 66
block scheduling, 14, 18
board of education, 6, 25, 59, 110, 115–
   16, 129, 137, 149–50, 159, 164
book fair, 153–55
boot camp, 1, 6, 23, 85–86, 174
Bryan, Ashley, vii–viii, 13, 26, 64–67,
   90, 172–73
budget cuts, 6, 25, 32, 59, 115–17,
   128, 149

bullying, 39, 43–44, 48, 135
bus driver, 34, 37, 93, 148
business involvement, 9, 36, 120,
   158, 160

cafeteria, 3, 15, 20, 24, 42–43, 63,
   66, 80–81, 90, 112, 126, 146, 156,
   158–61
careers, 9, 85
central office, 10, 33, 149–50
chaperoning, 33–38, 119–22
cheating, 21, 60, 104, 127
China, 40; Tiananmen Square, 87
circulating, 3, 23, 49
circus, 119–22
Civil Rights Movement, 107, 139
Civil War, 11, 53–57, 101–3
Clark, Joe, 6–7
classroom management, 3, 126, 146
Columbine massacre, 29, 126
Columbus, Christopher, 19
computers, 10, 20, 31–33, 60, 88–89,
   90, 117, 136, 164, 174
confrontation, 17, 91, 146, 148, 170
Cooper, Susan, 27
counseling, 4, 71
counterfeit money, 57
cubbies, 26, 82–84, 131, 146, 172

177

Curtis, Christopher Paul, 11, 106, 133–34, 138, 172
custodian, 21, 45, 73, 113, 160

deputy. *See* sheriff's deputy
differential attention, 60
disaffected youth, 6,, 60, 125
drugs, 38, 67–68, 75–76, 127, 135

English education, 10–11, 20–21, 60–62, 89, 97–99, 123–26, 163
exit exams, 17, 87
expulsion, 71, 79

field trip, 33–38, 118–21
fighting, 13, 38, 41, 42, 46, 50, 58, 69, 88–89, 143
fire, 82, 118
fishhooks, 35, 44, 173
football, 26, 40, 49, 69, 115
forgiveness, 169
foster parent, 25, 86, 109,
Freeman, Morgan, 7

G.E.D. *See* graduate equivalency diploma
gambling, 81
gangs, 34, 62, 67, 80, 95, 105
gentleness, 6, 71, 171
gifted education, 4, 163
Goodman, Greg, 33
graduate equivalency diploma (G.E.D.), 6, 86
graduate school, 11, 18, 89–90, 102, 163
graffiti, 2, 44, 82, 83, 143
guns, 21, 29, 31, 56, 62, 64, 81, 86, 93, 102–3, 118, 170, 173
gymnasium, 2, 24, 43–44, 49–50, 81–82, 91–92, 134–35, 144, 147–48, 157

Haberman, Martin, 3, 4, 147, 168–69, 174
head banging, 48, 77, 83

Hemings, Sally, 20
high expectations, 22, 169
Hine, Lewis, 61
history education, 11, 17–20, 53–58, 86–88, 99–103, 155–56, 163, 167–68
home visits, 3
homelessness, 75
Hughes, Langston, 66
human rights, 144
humor, 6, 173

India, 12
interrogation, 74–76
Iraq War, 62, 159

jail, 36, 44, 81, 85
Jefferson, Thomas, 19–20
judge, 9, 85–86, 129, 136

Kellmayer, John, 17, 26, 171
Kenya, 2, 40, 133, 138
knives, 39, 57, 59, 62, 68, 73, 80, 88
Kozol, Jonathan, 170
Kramer, Edith, viii

labeling, 69, 86, 131
Lee, Raymond, 130
L'Engle, Madeleine, 11
legislators, 9, 109–11
librarian, 6, 69, 86
lockdown, 29, 118
Loewen, James, 19, 62, 168
lunchroom. *See* cafeteria

Maine, 13
mainstream schools. *See* regular schools
medication, 20, 47, 83, 141; Ritalin, 16
Milwaukee, Wisconsin, 1, 4, 21
moonshine, 63
museum, 3, 4, 13, 139, 151

Navy, 11, 13, 107
Nigeria, 111
nurse, 6, 16, 25, 47, 49, 126

Ohio, 4; Cincinnati, 4, 86, 168
overcrowding, 7, 20, 24, 59, 74, 79, 116

parachute, 132–33
paraprofessional, 12, 13, 17, 25, 27,
    38–39, 41–42, 81, 92, 104, 111,
    114–15, 170
parent involvement, 3, 33, 71–72, 139
Parks, Rosa, 107
parole officer, 15, 16, 74, 89, 90–91,
    135–37, 140, 144, 159
Peck, Richard, 46, 172
Picasso, Pablo, 118
police, 29, 62, 68–69, 77, 118
poll patrol. *See* service learning
portfolios, 21
poverty, 3, 5, 43, 66, 70, 82
preschoolers, 24, 44, 72, 90, 130, 143
principal, 1–7, 12, 15–17, 24–26, 29–33,
    38, 42, 65, 67–77, 89, 116–18, 119,
    128, 135–37, 148–49, 153, 158–61,
    163
prison, 24, 71, 76, 86, 119, 135
promiscuity, 77, 94, 112
prostitution, 117

rampage, 29–30, 47,
Randall, Dudley, 139
reenacting, 11, 53–57, 102, 123
regular schools, 14, 26, 28, 33, 46, 61,
    116–17, 126, 130, 147, 163
restraint, 113
restrooms. *See* toilets
Robinson, Barbara, 172

S.O.S. *See* Save Our Students
S.W.A.T. team. *See* Special Weapons
    and Tactics team
Sachar, Louis, 106, 172
Save Our Students (S.O.S.), 24–26,
    68–69, 85–86, 109–11, 128–30,
    135–37
Scared Straight, 6
school board. *See* board of education

school bus, 34, 39, 82, 93, 108, 148
science education, 23, 58, 79–80,
    131–33
seclusion. *See* solitary confinement
senior citizens, 10
service learning, 9, 72
sexual harassment, 1, 11, 49, 77
sheriff's deputy, 25, 89, 91, 92, 100,
    106, 128, 136–37, 143, 157, 160
Sixteenth Street Baptist Church, 139
sleeping in class, 19, 31
snack machines, 59, 126, 147
solitary confinement cell, viii, 73–74,
    77, 111, 114, 171–72
South Africa, 64
special education, 12, 13–14, 26–28,
    38–51, 64–66, 82–84, 89–95, 103–8,
    111–15, 130–35, 138–40, 141–48 ,
    157
Special Weapons and Tactics team
    (S.W.A.T. team), 80
Spinnelli, Jerry, 27
stipends, 33
Stone Mountain, Georgia, 6, 27, 33–38,
    102
submarine, 11, 87, 101, 155
substitute teaching, 6,15,16, 38–51,
    89–95, 103–8, 127–28, 130–35,
    138–40, 141–48, 153–55
suicide, 30, 42, 95, 140
superintendent, 15, 11, 115–16, 145,
    149–50
suspension, 6, 20, 32, 47, 70, 88
swastika, 71

teacher appreciation day, 153–55
teacher of the year, 19, 161, 163,
    167–68
teen pregnancy, 14, 20, 135
terroristic threat, 1, 68
testing, 21, 44, 93–94, 134
textbooks, 62–64, 79–80, 113
theft, 157
toilets, 24, 29, 121, 146

tough love, 6
tribunal, 58, 79

urination, 50, 148, 173

vandalism, 1, 29, 44, 82, 112, 157
vocational education, 4

Washington, George, 19
water fountains, 44, 50, 92
Wiltwyck School, viii, 65, 173
worksheets, 26, 41, 76, 111, 142, 145
World War II, 58, 65, 102–3, 123

zoo, 3, 120, 121, 131–32

About the Author

Mary Hollowell is an associate professor of education at Clayton State University. Some of her articles on at-risk youth have appeared in the *American Indian Quarterly, American Secondary Education*, and *The High School Journal*. She will revisit Peachtree Alternative School teachers in a book chapter on therapeutic art and writing in Greg S. Goodman's forthcoming *Educational Psychology Reader: The Art and Science of How People Learn*.

Mary is a former public school science teacher and museum director of education. She has also worked for the National Park Service in Washington, D.C., at the Durrell Wildlife Conservation Trust in England, and in a marine biology lab in the Florida Keys. She lives in Peachtree City, Georgia, with her two daughters and tolerant husband, who always makes her laugh.